MORE NOTES FROM THE FIELD

SOUTHBOUND ON THE APPALACHIAN TRAIL AND OTHER JOURNEYS

KIRK WARD ROBINSON

HIGHLAND HOME

Nashville, Tennessee

BOOKS BY
KIRK WARD ROBINSON

NONFICTION

Founding Character:
Documents that Define the United States of America and its People

Founding Courage:
Courage and Character in the United States of America

Hiking Through History:
Hannibal, Highlanders, and Joan of Arc

Notes from the Field:
A Diary of Journeys Near and Far

More Notes from the Field:
Southbound on the Appalachian Trail and Other Journeys

FICTION

August Roads
Novellas

Life in Continuum
Stories

The Appalachian
A Novel

The Latter Half of Inglorious Years
A Novel

More Notes from the Field
Southbound on the Appalachian Trail and Other Journeys

A Highland Edition

Copyright ©2019 by Kirk Ward Robinson
All rights reserved, including the right of reproduction in whole or in part in any form.

Designed by Victoria Valentine
PageandCoverDesign.com

Printed in the United States of America

HighlandHome Publishing
Nashville, Tennessee
37215

ISBN 10: 0-9996042-4-4
ISBN 13: 978-0-9996042-4-3

Visit www.kirkwardrobinson.com

For Freewind

CONTENTS

PROLOGUE

2002
Hiking a Section of the Pacific Crest Tail
1

2016
Over the Alps from France to Greece
11

2016
A Sojourn on Nevis, West Indies
49

2017
The Sojourn on Nevis Continues
81

2018
Southbound on the Appalachian Trail
101

EPILOGUE
215

PROLOGUE

SATURDAY, MAY 18, 2019

Damascus, Virginia

Walking down East Laurel Avenue with Rocky, passing thru-hikers singly and in knots, many of them with the beginnings of beards, the women in braids, dreads or tightly woven rows, all burnished by weeks or even months in the outdoors, I search for that connection, that innate brotherhood engendered by strangers who meet one another in common calling on the Appalachian Trail.

"Are you okay?" Rocky asks.

She senses something but she isn't sure. She is, however, quite perceptive, because while I have hiked the Appalachian Trail three times, hauled myself over its gusting peaks, through its thickets of bear and biting insects, endured its mile after mile of stunning beauty and staggering hardship, I cannot now make that connection, be one with that brotherhood. You see, despite the 6000 miles I have trekked between Maine and Georgia, despite the highs and the hardships, today they are thru-hiking and I am not.

In all these years, eighteen since my first thru-hike, I have never been to Damascus, Virginia for Trail Days. The northbounders often spoke of it in shelter, with vivid reminiscences of an event which, undimmed by everything they had experienced since, had occurred months ago, a virtual eternity in trail time. For many southbounders—and all of my hikes have been southbound—Damascus, Virginia was a place we would eventually reach, but so unimaginably far from the Hundred-Mile Wilderness in Maine that we could only conjecture at its existence, like a land across an ocean. Trail Days was simply unattainable, and then after the trail, living so far away, it remained unattainable.

With the inevitable passing of seasons, so passed desire.

But something in me has changed. I completed my third thru-hike over seven and a half months ago. A winter has interceded, busy with restoration work on the old farmhouse, followed by spring's planting and pruning and making the orchards ready; and through all of these busy seasons, every single day of them, I have felt a physical need for the trail, a constant welling in my core, like the insistent hollow tingle sated only by sex. No night's desire can assuage this need, though, no tender touch. I am driven to go back but I am unable. There is much to do—much else to achieve—but there is this I can do: I can go to Trail Days, and I have.

I met Rocky yesterday at Grayson Highlands Inn, where I'm staying. She is a youthful year older than I, with a story that sometimes grinds down the emotions while at other times grates against them. But she is a thru-hiker right now, the Class of '19 if she completes her hike, which she seems perfectly bullish enough to do despite her ailments and mishaps. She completed the section between Damascus and Massie Gap day before yesterday, came in for a day of rest and has now stayed two. I know the feeling well. We've partnered up out of mutual need, I to vicariously relive the trail, she for shuttles into town and, I hope, good company.

The parade is going by as we eat lunch, the little restaurant packed with thru-hikers. We make extra room at our table for the brotherhood, or the sisterhood—call it the hood of hikers, then. Rocky is hiking this year, I am not. They gravitate toward her, I gravitate toward them, just to be a part of it, if only for a moment; but as deferential as they all are, I am not a part of it, not this year, and they know it.

Rocky and I will browse the vendors later, examine the latest gear. Perhaps she can yogi some things she needs. I don't need anything tangible myself, but maybe I'll meet someone I know, or knew, someone not on the trail this year. There I'll find a brotherhood I belong to, and then, if only for a short time, I can sate this driving desire, this need to move, to climb, to sleep under the sky. Maybe for a short time I can once again feel free.

SUNDAY, SEPTEMBER 29, 2019
Smith County, Tennessee

Yesterday is long ago and far away
I'm beginning to feel the years, but I'm going to be okay

Beginning to Feel the Years
Brandi Carlile

It has been a year to the day since I completed my last Appalachian Trail thru-hike. My desire to return to the trail has not dimmed, but a steady pragmatism has settled in, tempering that desire, keeping it manageable. Completing this book has also helped.

More Notes from the Field is a sequel to my previous travel collection *Notes from the Field* only insofar as today is sequel to yesterday: both stand alone but remain inherently connected just the same. While this new collection often refers to earlier journeys that I documented in the previous book, I believe I have added enough explanatory information to avoid confusion. You'll be fine if you read no further than this book, but consider taking a crack at the earlier book for the fullest experience.

I have used the same format as before, the datelined transcriptions from my travel diaries as well as the field notes I published on my website. I have edited freely to correct misspellings and mistakes, which are the reasonable result of writing fast on the fly. I have also changed the voice in some sections, so that my missives to myself, often in illegible handwriting, make sense to the reader.

And finally there is this: *Notes from the Field*, published in 2016, ended with the somewhat somber sense that my journeys were trickling to an end, that advancing age would soon confine me to the common. I did not wade in these despairing waters for long, as shortly after publication I was launched into journeys one after another that were as vibrant and authentic as any of my earlier adventures. The need to go and see transcends age, and as for the hardships along the way? Well, we are all tougher than we think.

I have proved it.

2002

SIERRA NEVADA
NATIONAL FOREST
North Fork
Prather
Bishop
John Muir Wilderness
NATIONAL FOREST
DEATH VALLEY NATIONAL PARK
KINGS CANYON NATIONAL PARK
Clovis
Fresno
Hume Lake
SEQUOIA NATIONAL FOREST
Independence
Forester Pass
Lone Pine
Mt Whitney
SEQUOIA NATIONAL PARK
Cottonwood Pass
Visalia
Hanford
Golden Trout Wilderness
Springville
SEQUOIA NATIONAL FOREST
South Sierra Wilderness
Porterville
Kennedy Meadows
Sherman Pass Rd
Chimney Peak Wilderness
Domeland Wilderness
Owens Peak Wilderness
Delano
Kernville
Onyx
Walker Pass
CALIFORNIA
Lake Isabella
Kiavah Wilderness
Ridgecrest
Bakersfield
Tehachapi Pass
Tehachapi
Mojave
LOS PADRES NATIONAL FOREST
Barstow
ANGELES NF
Vasquez Rocks Natural Area Park
Lancaster
San Gabriel Mountains National Monument
Pleasant View Ridge Wilderness
Agua Dulce
Saugus
Santa Barbara
Sheep Mountain Wilderness
Silverwood Lake State Rec Area
Wrightwood
ANGELES NATIONAL FOREST
Mt Baden-Powell
Lytle Creek
Skyforest
Big Bear City
SAN BERNARDINO NATIONAL FOREST
San Gorgonio Mtn
Oxnard
Pasadena
Arcadia
Glendora
Ontario
San Bernardino
Los Angeles
Riverside
CHANNEL ISLANDS NATIONAL PARK
Anaheim
Santa Ana
Mt San Jacinto State Park
Hemet
Idyllwild
Long Beach
CLEVELAND NATIONAL FOREST
SCALE 1:2,000,000
0 10 20 30 40 50 60 70 80 90 100 MILES
0 50 100 KILOMETERS
Oceanside
Escondido
Ramona
PACIFIC CREST TRAIL
NORTH
Alpine
Hauser Wilderness
San Diego
Tijuana

In the months after my 2001 Appalachian Trail thru-hike, I felt aimless and unfocused, cast adrift in a glaring, inauthentic world. I wouldn't come to understand post-trail depression—or the reasons for it—until much later. I had lost my position in Alaska, and couldn't seem to apply myself to anything concrete. I wandered across the country, dabbling at odd jobs, and eventually wound up at my friend Columbo's place in Santa Clarita, California. Columbo helped set me up with some temporary database work, which I could do alone and in the quiet of his home. I then spent the next few months working through my post-trail emotions until I felt confident enough to move on.

MONDAY, JANUARY 7, 2002

Santa Clarita, California

Worked five hours on the database. Not feeling great. I have that strange unmotivated feeling I had before I went on the AT. This is more than burnout, this is total dissatisfaction with the way things are going. I really need to join the Peace Corps or something.

SATURDAY, JANUARY 12, 2002

Santa Clarita, California

Another beautiful day. Can't just sit around. Drove out to the PCT trailhead and did some hiking. As it turns out, I hiked 16 miles, from San Francisquito Canyon Road north to Hughes Road, 8 miles each way. I feel pretty good. I just wanted to keep on going. Would have if I could have.

I can now say I have hiked on the Pacific Crest Trail.

MONDAY, JANUARY 21, 2002

Santa Clarita, California

Hiked 13 miles of the PCT today, from San Francisquito Canyon Road south to Bouquet Canyon Road. Couldn't get a hitch back to my car, so wound up doing a road walk of about another seven miles. A twenty-mile day in about six hours. Not bad, but I did get some blisters in the same old places: left heel, right ball, left little toe. There has got to be a way to conquer these blisters.

SATURDAY, JANUARY 26, 2002

Santa Clarita, California

Hiked 21 miles of the PCT today, from Bouquet Canyon Road south to Soledad Canyon Road, through Vasquez Rocks Park near where they used to film Star Trek, and through the tunnel under the 14 Freeway. Did the hike in seven and a half hours, but really tore myself up this time. Lots of blisters, even some new ones. Why would I get blisters in places I never got them before?

MONDAY, JANUARY 28, 2002

Santa Clarita, California

Three small earthquakes tonight. First I've felt since Alaska.

SATURDAY, FEBRUARY 16, 2002

Santa Clarita, California

Hiked round trip on the PCT today, 18 miles—Soledad Canyon Road south to North Fork Station. A little sore but feel pretty good. No blisters!

WEDNESDAY, FEBRUARY 20, 2002

Santa Clarita, California

Beautiful weather today. Hiked 11 miles round trip on the PCT, from North Fork Station south to Messenger Flats. I wish I could have gone farther. I wish I could just keep going.

SATURDAY, FEBRUARY 23, 2002

Near Mile 552, Pacific Crest Trail

Got my car moved to Green Valley, and then Columbo drove me up to Tehachapi so I could do another section of the PCT. Got on the trail about noon and hiked through fierce wind for about 12 miles before making camp. Walked among the wind turbines up there, even took shelter in one for a while. The door was ajar—the hatch, really—so I went in to get out of the wind. Whump, whump, whump, and so very still out of the wind. Whump, whump, whump—you hear it and feel it at the same time, reassuring for some reason. I could have slept right there.

SUNDAY, FEBRUARY 24, 2002

Cottonwood Creek, Pacific Crest Trail

For the record, there's no water in this dry wash called Cottonwood Creek.

Got on the trail about 8:30 a.m. No wind today, and had a great hike except no water anywhere. The sun is relentless. Getting low on water and getting worried when I found an unmarked stream at Tylerhorse Canyon. Thank God! Stopped for an hour, rehydrated and refilled my bottles. Pressed on 6 ½ more miles to Cottonwood Creek, a marked water source, but NO WATER.

Very tired, dehydrated, couldn't even eat.

MONDAY, FEBRUARY 25, 2002

Santa Clarita, California

Felt better this morning, but very low on water.

Hiked out of Cottonwood Creek toward Hwy 138. The "trail" is a dirt road paralleling the California Aqueduct for 16 miles. My water was gone by then and I hadn't peed in a while and I could hear the water rushing through the aqueduct pipe sounding clean and cold but I couldn't get to it. A spigot had a padlock on it. I wanted to scream.

Very hot and hard on the feet, and NO WATER.

Sunburned, dangerously dehydrated, just shuffling along and wishing I could take shade in my own shadow, which was the only shade around. Stop maybe? Crawl into the bivy to get out of the sun? Sure, and bake in there until you're tender and tasty, no way.

Staggering near Hwy 138. Don't know the time or the miles or the last time I drank water. Throat so dry I can't speak, only grunt as intelligibly as possible, and thank God there's a guy in an old truck doing something out here in the desert that I probably don't want to know about and I grunt and he gives me a ride to the Country Store on Hwy 138 and they've got a water hose and it takes a while but I finally put enough water in me and on me to cool down and be able to speak again.

I'm wiped, so I call Columbo, who comes and gets me and takes me back to Santa Clarita, a long drive, and I feel like road kill. Did I ever feel this bad on the AT? Probably, but it doesn't seem that way right now.

SATURDAY, MARCH 9, 2002

Near Bear Campground, Pacific Crest Trail

It's been a couple of weeks, my dehydration hike across the Mojave doesn't seem so bad now, the weather's great, so I got back on the trail.

Starting where I left off last time, I crossed Hwy 138 at 10:30 a.m., headed south on the trail and looked up at a wooded ridgeline that looms in startling contrast above the desert. I had climbs ahead, a couple thousand feet of them, but also trees, and trees mean shade. I'll gladly make the climbs in exchange for the shade.

As it turned out, the climbs were pretty easy. The grades out here are gentle compared to the AT, with switchback after switchback. Sometimes, though, there are so many switchbacks that you wish you could just cut up and make an AT climb…but naw.

Hiked about 16 miles and made camp. Great views back toward the desert. Really cold at night.

SUNDAY, MARCH 10, 2002

Santa Clarita, California

Woke up early, but it was so cold that I stayed in the bag until the sun was well up. Hiked about 15 miles through some pretty woods down to Lake Hughes Road, then five more miles of road walk to get to my car. This was a pleasant section with several water sources. A great day.

SATURDAY, MARCH 16, 2002

Santa Clarita, California

Went hiking on the PCT, 11-mile round trip from Messenger Flats to Big Buck Trail Camp and back. Not too strenuous, but damn cold up there above six thousand feet. I need to check, but I think I just hiked higher than I ever did on the AT…nope, not quite. Clingmans Dome is 6644 feet. I only went as high as Mt. Gleason at 6410. I'll be going above 9000 feet pretty soon, though.

WEDNESDAY, MARCH 27, 2002

Santa Clarita, California

Hiked the PCT today, about 13 miles round trip from Mill Creek Station to Road 4N24. Great weather, great hike.

SATURDAY, APRIL 6, 2002

Near Camp Glenwood, Pacific Crest Trail

Back on the PCT, and so damn glad to get away from Santa Clarita for a while.

Quite a few climbs today, but none of them tiring. A lot of springs through here. Finally, for the first time, I have hiked higher than the Appalachian Trail. Ridgetop Vista Point at 6760 feet. Well, not that much higher than Clingmans Dome, but still a first for me.

SUNDAY, APRIL 7, 2002

Little Jimmy Trail Camp, Pacific Crest Trail

Hiked 15 ½ miles today, and into elevation near 8000 feet. I have never hiked this high before. I've crossed the Angeles Crest Highway a couple of times, came around one mountain and got a view down to the city, mostly hidden by smog, the odd high-rise and antenna poking through here and there. It's blazingly clear up here, though.

I'm camping at 7400 feet. I feel weary, a little dizzy and beat up. Is it the elevation?

MONDAY, APRIL 8, 2002

Wrightwood, California

Only hiked 9 ½ miles today, but I went over Mt. Baden-Powell at 9245 feet and I have never been that high on foot! The views were exceptional, the air much clearer today.

TUESDAY, APRIL 9, 2002

Wrightwood, California

I love this town. I've been hanging out all day waiting for Columbo to come pick me up. I've enjoyed talking to the people here. I'm the only hiker in town. At mile 370 or thereabouts, I guess the northbound thru-hikers haven't made it this far yet.

This is it for me, then. I don't want it to end, but time has run out. I have a job interview in Raleigh, North Carolina next week, so it's time to pack up the car and go. I figure it'll take seven days to make the drive, plenty of scenery between here and there. I hope I can get back out here, though, and continue with the PCT. The few hundred miles I did just weren't enough.

2016

In the fall of 2015, I received an excited message from my friend Didier in France. I had met Didier in 2005 while doing research for the book that became Hiking Through History: Hannibal, Highlanders & Joan of Arc. *Didier runs a campground high in the French Alps, en route to a mountain pass that I believed Hannibal had used to invade Italy in the second century BCE. Because my research took me back and forth over the Alps several times, I was able to get to know Didier and call him a friend. He was nevertheless skeptical of my claims about Hannibal, which is why I laughed when I received his message. Archeologists, it seemed, had uncovered some potentially tantalizing evidence of Hannibal's march. Didier was now a true believer! He wanted me to come to his campground the following summer to give a lecture on Hannibal, which I was excited to do. I departed on this new adventure shortly after the publication of* Notes from the Field: A Diary of Journeys Near and Far.

FRIDAY, JUNE 24, 2016

Houston, Texas

Maybe I forgot how hot it gets here. Maybe I forgot how bad the traffic is. Regardless, my scotch over ice is cool.

I am on a roundabout road to France, via the Natchez Trace and Texas. It's been a pleasant trip so far, just the heat and the traffic &c. Driving the Natchez Trace was like a reunion. It's been nine years since my bicycle journey on the Trace, 900 miles round trip, plus another 700 from Houston to Natchez, Mississippi and back. Except for a long detour in Alabama due to repaving, some heavier traffic around Tupelo, and a complete bypass of Jackson, the Trace looks and feels exactly as it did last time. Indian mounds that had already aged multiple thousands of years have changed no further in these interceding few. I revisited the places I had camped back then, felt that I could have just forgone France and turned back for my bicycle right then.

Houston is the same only more so, hotter for sure, much more crowded, and now you have to pay tolls in order to cross town in a timely fashion.

But give it two more days...just two more days and I'll be out of this and on my way to Torino, Italy. For those who haven't followed, I'm heading to my friend Didier's campground in the French Alps, where I will be giving a lecture about Hannibal. I'm flying into Torino, Italy because, as counterintuitive as it might seem, flying there and then hiking over the Alps is actually the most efficient way to reach Didier's campground. Were I to fly into Paris, for example, I would then be faced with a journey by overnight train, linking with a regional train for a few more hours, a local bus for about another hour, and then a road walk of some miles. And this way I get to hike over the Alps again—geez, people go to Europe just to do that, so I surely won't complain.

Check back in a few days...

TUESDAY, JUNE 28, 2016

Torino, Italy

05:30...Why is it that the United States seems to be the only country in the world where you can get an essential cup of morning coffee without any nationalistic hassle to go along with it? I struggle with this everywhere in my travels, be it France, New Zealand, Germany, Norway, Italy...EVERYWHERE. Apparently, only in the United States has the crucial relationship between caffeine and waking up been made. Back home, coffee is coffee, available anywhere at any time, sometimes with half & half, with milk, or with "whitener," whatever the heck that stuff is. But the basic ingredient is coffee, offered in sizes designed to get the job done. It even works this way in the trendy, overpriced cafes, but go anywhere else in the world and you are forced to wade through myriad interpretations of coffee that seem to be set in nationalistic stone.

I had forgotten what a decent-sized coffee is called in Italy. That would be *cafe americano*, by the way, but for some reason I blurted, *cafe grande* as if I were in France, which seemed to enrage the dour fellow at the coffee machine. He threw up his hands, sputtered indignantly in Piedmont Italian, quizzed his line of effete espresso sippers, then eventually slammed an espresso on the bar like a whiskey in a western saloon. Torino is a cosmopolitan city so it was hard for me to consider that this guy had never encountered a tourist who needed more than a dollop of espresso to get the day going. Even were he an aficionado, why be rude? This wasn't the first time I had encountered this attitude, though, or the first country I had encountered it in. I downed the espresso in a single gulp, flipped a two-euro coin onto the bar, then went in search of friendlier surrounds.

I landed in Torino yesterday afternoon, took a bus from the airport to Statzione Porta Susa, where I intended to catch a train for the short ride to Pinerolo. From Pinerolo I could then take a bus a little farther on to the village of Bobbio Pellice, where I would find the trailhead for my hike over the Alps. I felt great coming off the plane, having scored a last minute upgrade for my flight to Europe, but jet lag set in by the time my bus arrived at Porta Susa, so that was that. I took a room in a nearby hotel, slept heavily until 3:00 a.m., felt as well and awake then as 8:00 p.m. back home (which it was), so that was that, too. I gnashed my teeth for two hours waiting for a cafe to open, and when one finally did I had to deal with the above.

Now to find another coffee joint, some place with bigger cups. Hurry...

TUESDAY, JUNE 28, 2016

La Monta, France

Same amazing day, much later—

I rocked that trail in 2005 at the age of 47; at 58 I had to work a little bit. I didn't remember the trail to Colle della Croce as being so steep, so long, and with those expansive views that forewarn every rocky step. I trudged along, two hours slower than last time, but then I made the col, tendrils of mist probing the rock faces. I took a long break in the lee of the old stone shelter, and knew with certainty that I would now be able to hike into Didier's campground while the sun was still high enough to light my reunion with special people and a special time.

And that's exactly how it went, although I felt a bit dislocated. The trail brought me out onto a road near the village of la Monta, rather than between the two houses in l'Eschalp as I was accustomed. That was the first strange thing, and then I couldn't spot Didier's rustic cooking shack. I sniffed the air for the aroma of his cooking, and that was absent as well. I continued along the road, some caravans beginning to appear through the trees to my left, the river Guil rustling beyond. Farther on there was a clearing where my memory told me the cooking shack should be, but I saw only some dome tents. Other buildings materialized, rustic in appearance but not the edifice I was searching for. There were more tents, a cluster of colorful caravans, and an office that definitely hadn't been here last time—*Accueil* (Reception)—and this confirmed that things had changed a lot in eleven years.

I found Didier in his cooking shack, which was much larger than before, so much so that I scarcely recognized the place. A tree was coming up through the middle of it, making me think that trees must really grow fast here since I remembered no tree from before. Didier had his back to me (perfect!), a pan in his hand, mushrooms swirling in butter and garlic. It smelled so good I didn't want to interrupt him, but I couldn't help but interject:

"So, the place looks very different but you look the same."

He turned to me then and his swarthy face brightened. "Solo!" he exclaimed, and in a moment he was out shaking my hand and I felt as welcome as if this were 2005.

What followed was a joyful reunion punctuated with sad tidings: Diclic, the old camp dog, was buried nearby; an avalanche had wiped out the campground in 2008, including the original Rustic Cooking as well as the approach trail I had hiked in 2005; and Carole had died in 2009. Didier had taken off some time to travel and heal after Carole's death, returning the following year to rebuild, improve and expand his operation. Today he has a new kitchen, a pair of yurts where he hosts fine dining, a rustic hot tub and sauna, kayaks, canoes, bicycles, and seasonal employees. People who are not guests still come for his meals or a glass of pastis in the evenings.

There is a new camp dog now, Jinka. She is as gentle and attentive as Diclic had been. It all feels different but the same. I feel right at home.

JULY 2, 2016

la Monta, France

Je m'appelle Kirk Ward Robinson. Je suis un ecrivain des etats-unis, mais mon francais est terrible, donc Chloe va traduire pour moi...

I memorized this and spoke it to a crowd of thirty or more people as an introduction to my lecture about Hannibal. I'm told I pronounced everything perfectly, although I think they were just being nice. Chloe Barret, a twenties-something polyglot from Aix en Provence who is helping Didier this summer, was my interpreter. Chloe is athletic, very pretty, and romantically committed elsewhere.

The purpose of my visit to Didier's campground in la Monta was to deliver this lecture, which went on for almost two hours. It was

The New Rustic Cooking

early evening, a bit windy and cool out, so we had moved the lecture into one of Didier's dining yurts. The yurts truly look as if they have been transported from the steppes of Mongolia, complete with the felt, although outfitted inside for fine dining.

Didier has become passionate about Hannibal, humorous in a way considering that he scarcely believed me when I told him eleven years ago that Hannibal had once come this way. I wanted to come through for Didier now, though. He had put a lot into this event, in materiel and personal capital. I was afraid the audience would be bored, having to wait for the translation, but Chloe played her part well. We even made them laugh a few times. I started out nervously, but once I was on a roll I let it all out with enthusiasm, often slipping into eager slang and dialect that stressed poor Chloe. The lecture was fun, and the audience clapped and asked questions afterward. Didier was pleased, I could tell by the satisfied sparkle in his dark eyes. I'm glad I came.

I think the best friendships are made this way, spontaneously, not requiring regular reinforcement. Now sitting under the trees, stars winking through the limbs, I drink a beer brewed here in la Monta and feel as if I am back in 2005, that there have been no interceding years. But there have been. I am older now and feeling it. Didier has a son now and another child on the way. Time moves on, although the view from where I sit hasn't changed at all.

I am faced with a dilemma. I could stay here all summer if I wanted, but Didier has a business to run, a business that runs mostly in French, a language that remains incomprehensible to me. With the time that I have, all of Europe is open for exploration. I'll need to give this some thought.

MONDAY, INDEPENDENCE DAY, 2016
la Monta, France

Every morning I sit on the steps of *Accueil*, the registration office, sip coffee and watch the sun crest the limb of a mountain across the way.

The air is chill, my breath drifts lightly and is gone. Except for a few questing birds, all is quiet and still. There is a high glow, like a distant fire, and then the sun erupts from one moment to the next, blinding, warm. My breath no longer steams. I take off my jacket. Another day gets under way.

I have been here a week now, long enough to establish a routine. In any of infinite alternate lives, I could live here and that would be fine. The reality is that I could extend my visa, stay the summer. Right now my farm seems distant, a memory, something of another time. Of course this sentiment will evaporate the moment I get home and see how much work I have ahead of me. But for now I count my blessings every morning that Didier was in his kitchen on that day eleven years ago, a rustic hamburger in the pan, the aroma of beef and garlic and onions wafting onto the road. If not for that I would have missed this place, wouldn't be here now. Chance encounters, the best kind.

Today I rolled up my sleeves and pitched in, beginning with potatoes, three varieties grown in this valley. They had to be washed, peeled and sliced; and then came the carrots, also three varieties, including a red carrot that I had never seen before. It has a tart taste, somewhat like a beet. Then Didier brought out three acorn squashes that he had cleaned and steamed, and these we filled with layer after layer of the three potato varieties, with sauteed cucumbers, squash, and onions sliced thin, a layer of tomatoes and then repeat until the squash was packed full. These went into a wood-fired oven where they were to cook all day. The dish is called *Tian Courgette Farcie*. We'll be sampling it later.

Now the sun is behind me and I can make out the etchings of a trail on the flank of my morning mountain. A steep hike but a perfect view. Maybe tomorrow.

Morning Mountain from Didier's Campground

TUESDAY, JULY 5, 2016

La Monta, France

It took a long, circuitous climb to reach the peak of my morning mountain, through tall grass that whipped me with dew, across sheep-cropped paddocks, and then finally into the tree line. The trail wasn't marked. Sometimes it would just fade out, as if erased from a blackboard. At other times it was indistinguishable from the sheep trails. I eventually cut my own switchbacks, aiming for a protrusion of rock high above, where I had made out the trail yesterday, just a winding scratch on the mountain from that vantage, fading along with the sun.

It was hardest in the trees, where I had no views and had to pull myself up from tree to tree in the steeper parts, navigating by instinct. One last hard pull brought me into a canted meadow, where the trace reappeared and I was able to follow it up and onto the ridge. I scrambled along the rocky ridge to the highest point, found a nook where I could sit out of the wind, and then just took it all in.

Mt. Viso stood in the distance to my left, at the head of the slender Valley of the Guil, its summit glittering with snow. If I was right, and if Hannibal had come this way, his army would have trekked up this valley like a crowded line of ants, the elephants breaking trail, and somewhere up there, behind a shoulder of snow-dotted stone, he would have found his pass into Italy. I had been unable to investigate that pass, the Col de la Traversette, in 2005 because it had been impassable, the snow too deep and dangerous. But now perhaps...I couldn't make out a trail from this distance, but I could clearly see broad expanses of bare rock with only slivers of snow. The col might be passable now. It was worth a call to the Mt. Viso refuge to find out. Didier would know how to reach them.

I settled back then, pleased with my new plan. I could see Didier's campground below, specks of activity, the silver-gray Guil, all so beautiful, so welcoming, so serenely fixed in place, but it was time to go.

But where?

Not knowing how long I would stay in France, I had scheduled my return flight for the first of August, still weeks away. The airline was Lufthansa, the return flight would be from Torino. So I could hike through the Col de la Traversette on my way back to Torino, that is if the col was passable, which would fulfill that missed goal from 2005. Then what? I could cross Italy easily enough, perhaps return to Passignano on Lake Trasimene to see if Marco was still running Camping la Spiaggia. It would be good to see Marco again.

Passignano was one of my favorite towns in Italy, perfectly located to get just about anywhere by train, and that's when I remembered the other missed goal from 2005. I had wanted to go to Greece. It would have been easy back then. While researching Hannibal in southern Italy, I had passed through the coastal town of Bari, where ferries run back and forth across the Adriatic. I had been running short of money, though, and still had to get back to France to do my research on Joan of Arc, so I had to abandon Greece. But now I could do it, so that was the plan.

I felt elated as I came down the mountain, parting herds of sheep along the way. Didier met me with a knowing smile and a glass of pastis. We sat at a cafe table under the trees.

"You have been up the mountain, yes?" he asked.

"Yeah," I sighed. "I could see you all down here. You're so lucky to have this place."

"It is true," he pondered, "but sometimes it is so much work and there is no time to climb the mountains."

I thought of my farm. "Yeah, I get that," I said, and then, like snapping off a bandaid to get it over with, I added, "I'm leaving tomorrow."

He nodded in thought, sipped his pastis. "Yes, this is the way you are. I knew it would be soon."

"I hate to go."

He shrugged his shoulders. "Yes of course, but you like to walk on the mountains, not to only look at them. We will be here when you come again."

He hauled himself up, patted me on the shoulder, then lumbered to his kitchen to begin dinner.

WEDNESDAY, JULY 6, 2016

Pian del Re, Italy

Bouncing up a narrow track in a Range Rover that looks the part, terminal drops just over my right shoulder, Sarah explained to me some of the challenges of managing the Mt. Viso refuge.

"Sometimes we get helicopter drops of supplies," she said, "but these are expensive. We mostly pack everything in. I had one thought that the hikers coming up could each bring something, but we've never found a way to make that work."

Sarah is an engaging woman, fit, and may be French or English. As she switches between languages, her accent switches as well. Sarah is what we would call on the Appalachian Trail a *hut master*. Her challenges are no different than those faced at Lakes of the Clouds Hut on Mt. Washington, except that here we are a couple thousand feet higher.

The track ends at a primitive parking area above the tree line and we get out to hike the final kilometers. This will take about an hour

Mt. Viso

of steady ascent, but before we reach the refuge we will part, she to the right, I to the left toward Col de la Traversette. Sarah isn't sure if the col is passable. She was just there on Saturday and the snow was still pretty deep. It's been a warm few days, though. I might be able to make it. We say our goodbyes under an expansive blue sky, craggy peaks above. If I can't make it, I say, I'll backtrack to the refuge. Perhaps I'll see her later. If not, *au'revoir* and *merci beaucoup*.

I climb quickly into a lunar landscape, rocky, gray, but with water dripping everywhere. These are the headwaters of the river Guil, which rushes past Didier's campground in a torrent. I stop to drink the water. It is cold and pure. Alpine flowers sprout from cracks, colorful evidence of the tenacity of life, but soon even these are below and behind me. Lichen paints the rocks in orange and yellow brush strokes, as if drawn by hand.

I stop every so often to catch my breath in the thinning air, to spy a field of slushy snow ahead. I tramp through the snow, taking the footsteps of others. The snow is mostly firm, but then I plunge to my hips. My trekking poles cannot find a bottom. Freeing myself

Col de la Traversette

without leverage requires that I embrace the snow and scoop it to my chest, swimming in a way. I manage to free myself and continue on, soaked and cold although I dry out quickly in the unblemished sun.

The final push to the col takes all I have. This is not a technical climb, just a steep, steep hike. When I lift myself over the last rocks, Italy comes into view, broad and clear and mountainous, a postcard of infinite space. I have to pause to catch my breath, and not because of the exertion or thin air. The view is simply stunning.

Now I am at the headwaters of the mighty river Po. I drink some of this water on my way down a trace of trail scratched from bare rock, twisting and turning in tight hairpins. I'm glad I'm going down and not up. It takes a couple of hours to get down to Pian del Re, a family-run refuge, more like a rustic hotel. It's about 17:00. There is no Wi-Fi at the refuge. They do not take credit cards, only cash, of which I have none. I practically wilt where I stand, coated in sweat salt, sunburned, my legs trembling. I must look pitiful because the woman gives me a room anyway, says we can figure out how to pay for it later.

I mutter grateful thanks, head for a hot shower and a warm bed while the sun dips behind Mt. Viso, drawing a shade on Pian del Re.

FRIDAY, JULY 8, 2016

Yesterday—
1. A guy from Pian del Re drives me to the town of Paesano
2. I miss the bus so must take a taxi to the town of Saluzzo
3. I take a bus from Saluzzo to Torino Piazza Carducci
4. I take the subway from Torino Piazza Carducci to Porta Susa
5. I take a train from Porta Susa to Firenza
6. I take a train from Firenza to Terontola
7. I take a train from Terontola to Passignano

Geez! This trek was as tough as yesterday's climb!

An ATM in the village of Crissolo took care of my bill at the refuge. I had intended to walk from there, but the kind old man who drove me from Pian del Re took me on down to Paesano where I could catch the bus. The old fella couldn't speak English but understood my thanks just the same. I missed that bus because I was one step too slow. The doors closed just as I reached the bus, and despite eye contact with the driver, the doors did not re-open. Okay, this happens sometimes.

It was past noon by the time I reached Torino, but the train schedules lined up and soon I was clacking along the foot of the Apennines on my way to Passignano and its famous lake. I arrived too late to walk across town to see if Marco still runs Camping la Spiaggia, so I took a room in town, had a meal of gnocchi with eel, along with lake perch in truffle sauce, and too much wine.

The morning has dawned clear and cool. Now to find Marco.

SATURDAY, JULY 9, 2016

Ancona, Italy

My visit with Marco was pleasant. He didn't remember me at first, although to me he looked exactly the same. Once I reminded him of Hannibal, though, as well as *birra fredda americano*, *Solo*, and a few other key words, he came around with sudden recognition, smiled wide and shook my hand. I marveled at his campground. Like Didier, Marco has been busy. It turns out that when I met him in 2005 he had only been into his second season with the place. Now, after a decade, he has improved it considerably, with a bonafide restaurant, swimming pool, umbrella chairs along the shore, and a well-stocked bar. And the beers were even cold! The place was packed with caravans and tent campers, still plenty of room for me to pitch my tent but it felt too crowded. Plus Marco was busy riding herd on all of this, so I shook his hand once more, bid him *arrivederce*, and headed for the train station.

Along the way I went into a travel agent for help with a ferry to Greece. This proved to be prescient because I would never have figured it out on my own. What I found online was a chaotic swarm of mixed information, almost entirely useless. There are so many ferry companies, so many ports, and so many scams. I had decided to take a train to either Bari or Brindisi, near the heel of Italy, the two closest ports to Greece. I had been to Bari during my Hannibal trek so knew the lay of the land. From there I expected to be able to find a ferry company easily enough, pass them some euro, then climb aboard.

The travel agent, who spoke charmingly flavored English, had a better plan. He set me up quickly and efficiently with Anak Lines, departing from Ancona, which is on the north Adriatic coast only a couple hours by train from Passignano—much closer than Bari—and bound for Patras in the Peloponnese, a good jumping-off point to explore north toward Athens. I have been to Ancona before as well, so had no worries navigating the trains.

I arrived in Ancona at about 17:00, still Friday the 8th. The sun was as yet high, although late enough that a full day's haze lay over the city and port. It was hot and loud. I didn't remember Ancona as being so large. I took off at a fast clip along the waterfront hoping to find an inexpensive hotel. Any campgrounds would be out of town, and I didn't want to risk getting too far away from the docks where my ferry would depart.

Reaching a hotel required climbing seemingly endless steps through tight alleys. Occasionally a Vespa scooter would flit past, but the alley was too narrow for cars. Even now I don't know how people in cars reach the hotel. Nevertheless I got there, got a room for a decent price, then went in search of food. The last time I had eaten was at Marco's campground, and that was only a brioche, and that was eleven hours ago. I was starving, of course—and no, I couldn't find any food. I did find an outdoor eatery in the Piazza J.F. Kennedy, but regardless whom I flagged, how pitiful and starving I looked, received no information on how to sit and order food. Same old problem. The bakeries were all closed, or else a sack of brioche would have sufficed as before, so I found a shop and made due with some peanuts and chips.

Morning coffee...I shake my head. The hotel put on an impressive breakfast buffet, gratis, with every kind of juice imaginable; with eggs, sausage, bacon, brioche, cheese, cold cuts, cucumbers, bell peppers, tea—all the usual European stuff, but a cup of coffee had to be hand-made with pride, cost a couple of euro, and could be drunk in one gulp. This is like quenching a hot day's thirst with an ounce of a beer that costs three dollars! The next time I come I'm bringing instant. Hot water from the tap will do in a pinch.

Off in search of ferry check-in, my morning shower is quickly wasted. It's hot, man, and nothing makes sense. Roads and train tracks garrison the waterfront, and yet somewhere in there is an office I must find. It is a chaos of traffic, visually confusing. A lady at the hotel had given me directions. Twenty minutes, she said. Her directions collapsed at the first traffic-circle intersection. I found boats aplenty, fishing boats, shirtless crews with bronzed skins bending over nets and ropes, preparing to disembark for the day. Cigarettes dangled from lips that spoke Italian and Greek, perhaps simultaneously.

I must have prised out every dank, hidden corner of Ancona's waterfront, but with tenacity and sweat did eventually find my boat. *Hellenic Spirit* sits at anchor as the day goes long. Departure is overdue. That's okay, my Mythos beer is cold, and I'm cool in this scrap of shade.

SATURDAY, JULY 9, 2016

Aboard H/S/F Hellenic Spirit

Later—

After two tall beers and a bottle of wine I am feeling pretty resilient. This boat crawls. I am in a cabin with four bunks—okay, it's like an overnight train in France, but if I had gone for standard seating during this twenty-one-hour crossing I would be like the people on Deck 8, the ferry equivalent of economy class. People are literally camped out on the deck. They are lying there, holding sheets or cardboard over their heads to block the sun. Some have pitched

HFS Hellenic Spirit

tents, arrayed as if this were a floating campground. Others are on air mattresses. Little children run about bare-assed. Chiseled guys have stripped to their shorts. Foreign backpackers huddle in shaded corners, their gear spread around them like litter. It seems so...damn, it seems so *third world*.

There is usually a plaque at reception, often bronze, mounted with some flourish and displayed with pride, and this plaque gives the ship's official designation and launch date. Not so here. I asked a purser what the ship's designation was, and he didn't know. He did not seem put out, he wasn't indignant—in truth he became quite curious.

"I do not know this," he said. "It is strange but I have never thought of this."

After some research he tracked it down for me, informed his fellow crew in Greek in a tone that seemed to impart a kind of mystified dumbfoundedness.

"Here, it is H/S/F," he said. "Now I have learned something, too."

And what does H/S/F stand for? He shrugged his shoulders; damn, a new mystery. "*Hellenic Spirit Ferry*," he hypothesized with a shrug, and I let it go at that.

Otherwise the Adriatic Sea looks like the Gulf of Mexico on a languid summer day, placid, boundless, and with no land in sight. The best value at the bar is beer or ouzo. The whisky costs too damn much.

SUNDAY, JULY 10, 2016

Parga, Greece

Yes, they are staring at you: cafe sitters furtively from behind their sunglasses, shy kids spying from second floor windows, and taxi drivers directly. You're outside of the route, the well-acquainted tourist path. You are an enigma, an outlier. The cowboy hat doesn't help.

The crowding onboard *H/S/F Hellenic Spirit* (HSF for *High Speed Ferry*, takk to my European researcher) just about did me in. I escaped to my communal cabin shortly before sunset, hoping to find some quiet, and blessedly the cabin was empty, my mates out yonder

GREECE
KORÇE
Bilisht
Kastoriá / Καστοριά
THESSALONÍKI / ΘΕΣΣΑΛΟΝΙΚΗ
Corovodë
Ersekë
Përmet
GJIROKASTËR
Véroia / Βέροια
Peraia / Περαία
Kalamaria / Καλαμαριά
Kozáni / Κοζάνη
Kateríni / Κατερίνη
Ioánnina / Ιωάννινα
Tríkala / Τρίκαλα
LÁRISA / ΛΑΡΙΣΑ
Kardítsa / Καρδίτσα
Makrinitsa / Μακρινίτσα
Parga
Πάργα
Arta / Άρτα
Vólos / Βόλος
Preveza / Πρέβεζα
Lamía / Λαμία
Lefkáda / Λευκάδα
Thermopylae
Agrinio / Αγρίνιο
Náfpaktos / Ναύπακτος
Leivadeia / Λιβαδειά
Chalkída / Χαλκίδα
Mesolóngi / Μεσολόγγι
Argostóli / Αργοστόλι
Aígio / Αίγιο
MER EGÉE
PÁTRA / ΠΑΤΡΑ
Kórinthos / Κόρινθος
Elefsína / Ελευσίνα
Ilio / Ίλιον
ATHENS
PEIRAIÁS / ΠΕΙΡΑΙΑΣ
Glyfáda / Γλυφάδα
Zákynthos / Ζάκυνθος
Amaliada / Αμαλιάδα
Pýrgos / Πύργος
Trípoli / Τρίπολη
Náfplio / Ναύπλιο
Pylos / Πύλος
Kalamáta / Καλαμάτα
Spárti / Σπάρτη
Methóni / Μεθώνη
Monemvasia / Μονεμβασία
Kýthira / Κύθηρα
Réthym

somewhere. I climbed into my upper bunk for a short nap, and awoke eight hours later to an insistent knocking at the door. It was dark in the cabin, just a sliver of light coming from under the bathroom door. My cabin mates lay under twisted blankets. One of them rose, rubbed his forehead and muttered something in Greek. I remembered the authority of that knock from my voyage aboard *MV Galaxy* a decade ago. It was time to disembark.

The line at the coffee bar was long. Something had happened to the hot water, so only iced coffees were available. I ordered one and downed it with a grimace, grabbed my backpack and huddled in the disembarkation line with the others. *Hellenic Spirit* clanked and groaned up to the pier, and then we all moved in a shuffling file, weary, a bit smelly, babies squalling.

08:00 hours and it was already hot. It seemed too early in the voyage to be disembarking, but passengers were crossing the ramp and fanning out, cars sprinting down the ramp beside them and then across a bare concrete apron larger than a football field.

Man, it was hot!

There were no buses, no shuttles. People congregated in groups as if something were going to happen. I watched for a while, searching for clues, then slung my backpack and took off in the direction the cars were going. I must have walked a good half mile, looking over my shoulder from time to time. No one else was walking, not even the grubby backpackers. Something was wrong. I rounded some buildings, saw that the cars were sprinting onto a busy highway with no sidewalks, nowhere to walk. I could make out rooftops above the aggregation of administrative buildings in front of me, perhaps hotels, maybe tourist information if I were lucky. But to get there...

I passed under awnings, around corners; I cut through a line of shrubs. I was circling a port terminal and disembarkation lounge, although both were closed, dark. Nevertheless, out front sat two taxis. One of the drivers approached me.

"Where you go?" he asked. He looked at me as if I were not quite sane.

"A hotel? Tourist information?" I muttered in return.

"You do not have this here," he said. "This is a port. It is not a place for tourism. I take you to Parga, nice beaches, good hotels. That is a place for tourism."

Now that I had worked my way around the terminal I could see that I was trapped behind a busy highway. I wasn't going to be able to make it on foot so I took him up on his offer. Anything to get out of there.

His name was Villiers. His talkative manner and practiced English reminded me of Martin, the taxi driver on Madeira back in 2005. We shot quickly away from the port, climbed past groves of olives and citrus. The road became narrow, isolated, bordered by brush, and it crossed my mind that Villiers might not be a taxi driver at all but a robber. We topped a rise, though, and there was a town ahead, so I let those thoughts drift away.

"How do you pronounce Patras correctly?" I asked him, emphasis either on first or second syllable.

"What?" he asked, flummoxed. "You are not coming from Patras, you are coming from Igoumenitsa."

"*What?*" my turn, and then I realized—I had disembarked about five hours early, and nothing, *nothing*, onboard would have clued me otherwise, not the crew, not a sign, not an announcement—nothing.

I thought to be angry, but then what was Patras to me? Just a place in Greece, no more recognizable than this. So after our revealing drive, Villiers brought me into the seaside village of Parga, showed me around, pointed out the bus stop and a few reasonably priced hotels. He taught me some words in Greek, how to say please and thank you and so on.

Parga is a steep town, like a spread of colorful jam on an uphill piece of toast. The Ionian Sea is down there, a sparkling sapphire with a pretty beach. The hotels are cheaper at the top of town. I am in Hotel San Nectarios, having shown up at just the right time to score room 7, the penthouse with its extraordinary view.

You know, I might just stay a couple of days.

Parga

MONDAY, JULY 11, 2016

Parga, Greece

If only you could see what I see. Photos do not do it justice: a lavender sunset, neon and stucco and red clay tile, lights ringing the ancient fortress, a lone paddle-boarder in the inky Ionian. Lights flicker on, girls giggle below, somewhere drums are beating. What I love about these coastal European towns is that just when you think you have the lay of the land, you turn left and discover something new.

    I discovered a restaurant while essentially lost, the Taka Taka Mam, with a proprietor couple so enterprising as to stand in the narrow cobbled street and rope people in. That's how they got me, and the food was great. Last night I had lamb; tonight I had swordfish. I stayed there long after I had finished my swordfish, my wine and my espresso—it was a joy just to watch those two work. An accidental journey, the best kind. And now I have new friends. As so often happens, I felt I could stay here and be happy, or as I wrote in my journal, *what a great way of life for people who can sit still.*

I leave early tomorrow for Athens. It will be before midnight for most of you. I depart with sadness but also the excitement of new discovery. Trying to reschedule my return flight, Lufthansa has proved to be as incompetent as American air carriers. I'll try to work it all out in Athens. In the meantime, if I get another chance to travel to Parga, to stay at Hotel San Nectarios and eat at Taka Taka Mam, I will feel privileged for the opportunity.

WEDNESDAY, JULY 13, 2016
Athens, Greece

Okay, I have seen it, the original as well as the fake one in Nashville, along with the stellae in the British Museum; and on top of that I have completed the Grand Tour. Now to absent myself from this place with all dispatch.

Athens is not for me. I am loathe to criticize another city or country while I am in it, but I don't feel a harmonic in this place. One could possibly carve out an interesting experience in a small grid of streets, under cafe umbrellas and olive trees, with familiar landmarks within view, but the breadth of this city is like trying to navigate Houston, Texas on foot. It can't be done, or else would require a lifetime to ferret out its better places.

And it's hot, man—it's hot.

I disembarked after seven hours by bus from Parga at a sprawling bus station yesterday afternoon at 15:00 local, thought I could just walk out of there but was disabused of that notion the moment I stepped outside, where encircling highways held me as if in a corral. As it turns out, I either was or was not anywhere near the city center. I prevaricate because I received conflicting information. I was at Terminal B, either close to the city center or else in suburbs many kilometers away. It depended upon whom I asked. My map of Athens was no help. One person sited us off the map, another closer in. I was instructed to take a bus, #51, which would carry me to Omonia Square (pronounced like *ammonia*), near the city center, hotels, &c. I

Athens

bought a ticket for €1.50, hopped aboard and, an hour later, wound up way off and gone at the Athens airport!

Geez! Buses. Damn!

I took advantage of this to try to communicate with Lufthansa Airlines about my return flights, got blown off with indignity and indignation, hailed a taxi driver named Stefanos and bid him get me the hell out of there.

To his credit, Stefanos was very helpful. He charged me only the city-mandated €38 for the ride, found a hotel for me (Hotel Minoa), waited to be sure I could get a room, then gave me a quick tour of the area. He warned me away from Omonia Square due to the refugee influx. Nice guy. But beyond that I was exhausted, so went to my room and collapsed.

This morning I sought out one of the most famous sites of antiquity, the Acropolis. At various places one can see it at the end of long avenues, but not from the warren I inhabited. My map wasn't much help since, while most street signs are in Greek although also with a phonetic rendering, most of the streets did not have street signs. I had given away my compass in France as a gift, so I took a bearing from the morning sun and set out—and within half a sweaty hour found the place.

Entry was €20 although I paid €30, €10 extra for some bonus feature I have yet to identify. Perhaps I passed it without realizing, nevertheless I paid my €30 and went for a stroll through the Golden Age of Pericles. But for the crowds, the place had a weight of history unequaled anywhere else in the world, notwithstanding Rome. The views alone are stunning, the ruins of the Parthenon, Temple of Aphrodite, &c. like an added attraction. A massive restoration is underway to correct slights both ancient and modern. This place hasn't seen much peace since about 400 BCE or so.

Acropolis

MORE NOTES FROM THE FIELD | 37

Temple of Aphrodite

Parthenon

What surprised me the most was the sheer scale of the site. I had no idea it was so large, and with so much layered history, of Greeks and Romans and Byzantines and Ottomans, not to mention the British. Circumnavigating the base of the Acropolis, I saw etchings and carvings in the rock that might have gone back to the Stone Age. Its commanding heights and natural springs would have made the Acropolis an important site into pre-antiquity, so it's no wonder that Athens was founded here.

Back to the present, keeping the sun to my left returned me to my hotel, a journey that shocked my senses. There is trash everywhere, graffiti on everything, even on the trash, and buildings vacant and crumbling. Wet clothing, hanging in trees to dry, drips yellowish, acrid liquid onto the sidewalks. Crossing a street takes some daring and planning. It is almost wounding to see the birthplace of western civilization in this condition.

But then, across the way, a street bizarre is going on. I saw a booth that displayed a dozen or more olive varieties in bulk, just pick and choose, and they smelled wonderful; then fish, and every fruit imaginable. A pita gyro, enough calories to last a day, costs only €2.50, and a beer large enough to swallow an English pint costs only €3. *Efharisto*, thank you, I think I'll order another.

THURSDAY, JULY 14, 2016

Kaumeda Vouvla, Greece

That's the Chalkidian coast over there, the long barrier island that rises from the surf in layered mountains, guarding Attica's sea approaches. It's why Xerxes landed where he did, hence the famous battle. The view is magnificent.

Before that view, though, there was supposed to be a bus that would take me from my hotel in Athens to Terminal B, but, uh, well, buses… So I hoofed it, forty-five minutes getting lost, and then another forty-five minutes to actually get there. Again the sun was more help than my map, just kept my bearing north, and once I cleared some locally confusing streets packed with traffic, I found my road and arrived at the station with fifteen minutes to spare.

A three-hour bus journey deposited me at Thermopiles, as dry, dusty and hot as any chaparral town along the upper Rio Grande. Man, it was hot. No one spoke English—there wasn't even a cafe— and wherever the heck Leonides might reside was incomprehensible. Were there buses, taxis, a hotel? These questions were lost on the locals, and I do have a phrasebook. Could I possibly be the only English-speaking person who ever journeyed here to see the site of the famous Battle of Thermopylae? It seemed not possible, but to these folks I could have been from the moon.

Getting late and hotter yet, I shouldered my backpack and began the trek south to the next town, Molos, where I hoped to find a hotel and perhaps someone who spoke English. Five road-walking miles and a rising blister later, I reached Molos, which at least had a cafe although the proprietor spoke no English. There was no hotel in the town. I know because I walked every street in search, lifting that blister even higher. No more walking, I located the bus terminal, mimed my needs, and received a bus ticket to the coastal town of Kammena Vourla.

The bus took only minutes to get here, while walking would have taken me two hours. I put in at the Hotel AKTH along a pretty strand, showered as if I were just off the Appalachian Trail, then of course went for a beer. For food I ordered fried cheese. This came in a piping hot dish, goat cheese fried along with tomatoes and bell peppers in aromatic olive oil. It smelled and tasted wonderful, and although this was actually an appetizer, it was enough to fill me up even after all the hiking I had done.

Tomorrow I will take the bus back to Thermopylae (Thermopiles) to find the site. I know the place will look nothing like it did during the battle—I suspect even the Alamo might not look like much after 2496 years—nevertheless I still want to go if only to stand on the ground where history was made. When I was there earlier, I spied a hulking mountain to the north that came down close to the water. That must be the place. Centuries, nay millennia, of sedimentation have moved the shore out by a couple of kliks. Nothing will resemble antiquity except the mountains...except the mountains.

FRIDAY, JULY 15, 2016

Thermopylae, Greece

Just because I travel alone and there are no witnesses doesn't make me any less foolish. Yesterday, if I had walked north along that hot, dusty highway for 300 more meters, around a slight bend and beyond those scrappy bushes, I would have found it. In yesterday's heat, and after that long bus ride, I simply gave up too soon.

I realized that as I wheeled in on the place this morning, slapped my head and massaged my aching foot. It was the mountain I had seen, I knew it, and upon closer inspection I could visualize it all. Everything made sense, even after 2496 years. The waves would have washed past where I now stood, lapping at the feet of the hills to my left. There's what looks like a gorge in those mountains, actually a defile between the mountain and a hill, the only way to pass back then, the Hot Gates, so named because of a nearby hot sulfur spring. You've probably seen the movie, *The 300*, so I don't need to describe the battle. The movie is fiction, yes, but as accurate as anything else we know for sure, which from such antiquity is little more than myth itself.

Regardless the finer details, something big did happen here in 480 BCE. I can sense the very weight of it—geez, I get wishy-washy about this stuff. The Spartans did stand and fight—this is fairly certain— and their story has survived. It should be noted that from Darius to Xerxes, the Persian Empire was defeated or diverted at each invasion, at places with memorable names: Plataea, Marathon, Artemesium, and of course, Thermopylae. Greek history would not go calmly on. The Golden Age of Pericles fell within a generation, then the Peloponnesian War so weakened Athens and Sparta that, while Sparta won the first round, all of them eventually fell. Alexander of

Leonides Monument, Thermopylae

Macedon became preeminent, but his was a bright, short flame. By the time of Hannibal, two centuries later, Rome had dominion over Greece. What would Leonidas have thought about that?

There is nothing ancient at the site except the mountain and the spring. There are olive groves where the sea once washed ashore, hot, chalky soil, very little shade. Has the climate changed since then? Probably. Maybe the trees were taller, a forest instead of scrub. Or maybe it looked just like this.

The museum is an oasis, staffed by a pair of friendly and enthusiastic women who speak English. They spun up a short film for me, in Greek but with English subtitles. I was so moved I wanted to buy the soundtrack. They looked at one another oddly, as if mulling, *Why didn't we think of that?* I'll keep an eye on their website, maybe a soundtrack will show up.

At last the monument itself, which is rather recent as well. My old history books spoke of a stone with the inscription, *Go tell the Spartans, passerby, that here by Spartan law they lie.* I asked the two women about this. They shook their heads together. The stone wasn't ancient, did not date to that period, and whatever its provenance, is no more. But the monument has an impact, a memorial wall, Leonidas on a pedestal with his javelin raised, the 300 represented by a single Spartan below and to each side. There is another monument, also modern. It resembles a memorial cairn, although the bones it would hold are atoms now.

The hot spring deserves another look, so I might return tomorrow. The water is showerhead hot, and the sulfur is said to have healing properties. I might just dip in my feet.

SATURDAY, JULY 16, 2016
Kammena Vourla, Greece

A spoon will almost stand up in a cup of Greek coffee, and what the Greeks can do with a waffle is amazing. They take what is a standard round waffle, smother it with two kinds of cheese, tomatoes, peppers

Kammena Vourla

and corn, bake it and serve it up. Even after burning several thousand calories the past couple of days, I couldn't finish mine. Between Didier's cooking and the rich food in Greece, I might actually gain weight on this trip.

Mornings laze up gently here. I have been awake since sunrise, but only now, at about 09:00, has traffic begun to pick up on the road that parallels the strand. The boats aren't moving yet, and I only see one swimmer in the surf. The language all around me seems to be exclusively Greek, no other tongues that I can detect, so this must be a Greek place to take holiday, far from the more crowed international destinations. I had a feeling it would be this way. Greece has so much coastline, between the mainland and the islands, that you could probably send all of Europe on vacation here and still find long stretches of isolated beach, or else places like this. For some Greeks, perhaps this place is an escape from the clamor of foreign tongues.

What I have yet to master is how to pay for my meals and drinks. What I mean is, table service is always prompt. Afterward, though, the waiter never returns. I watch the others—what do they do? People sit for hours it seems; I have yet to observe anyone else paying their bill. So I will eventually get up, track down a waiter, and mime for the bill. This is always met with a nonplussed look, the ignorance of foreigners or some such, but I don't know what else to do.

I have a couple more days here. I had originally thought to get out to some of the islands, especially Santorini (Thera), where it is thought a volcanic eruption in 1628 BCE or thereabouts, perhaps the largest in recorded history, brought about the downfall of the Minoan civilization, influencing mythologies from Greece to Egypt. Earthquakes, fires in the sky, tsunamis that could have parted seas, and with the death and pestilence that would have followed, certainly lend to the basis of western mythology, especially the biblical stuff. Unfortunately, the costs of mistranslation prevent this, and I depart for Norway on Monday anyway.

I'm not disappointed. Santorini probably looks pretty much like this. But what to do for the next two days? I could go swimming in the surf, I guess, but I didn't bring swimwear. The Greeks don't seem to go naked the way the rest of Europe does, so I can't get away with that. The water looks so cool, though. I need to think of something, maybe cut off the legs of my base layer. Yeah, I'll work it out.

SUNDAY, JULY 17, 2016

Kammena Vourla, Greece

A few final words from Greece, and to note that my spellings have been all over the place. I have seen Kammena also spelled *Kamena*, and I have seen Thermopylae spelled also as *Thermopiles* and *Thermopylis*. This would be on actual Greek signs, so I don't know which is correct. I have, therefore, tried to account for all varieties.

Tomorrow morning at 05:00 I begin an arduous journey to Athens Eleftherios Venizelos Airport, which will begin with a three-hour bus ride to Terminal B followed by an hour's ride on bus X93 to the airport itself. I have decided to fly to Norway to see my friend Gunnhild. I should have plenty of time to make my flight to Oslo, but then, well...let me tell you about the buses.

I watched the sunrise this morning, the breeze was cool enough to be inspiring, and I felt an urge to brave a return to Thermopylae for a more in-depth investigation. I finished off my double espresso—about the largest coffee you can get here—hoofed around the cove to the bus station and bought a ticket for the 09:30 bus. Easy enough, the ticket was only a couple of euro, and when the 09:30 bus arrived I climbed aboard.

I knew I was in trouble when the bus turned left at the highway instead of right. Sweat popped out on my forehead. *Hellig ku*, I was going the wrong way! I signaled the conductor, who examined my ticket with raised brows.

"Wrong bus," he said, although I had not signaled in any way that English was my predominate language. I expected a firestorm, but he smiled: "No problem, no problem. We stop you in Agios Konstantinos (another town a little way down the road). You change bus. No have to pay more."

He said all of this with a reassuring smile, even patted me on the shoulder. "All okay," he said. "All okay."

My new bus station was blessedly shaded, so I settled in for the forty-five-minute wait for the next bus, which arrived right on time. A man came sprinting out of the bus station, pointing at me and then the bus. "This is for you," he said. "Bus to Thermopyles." He went on to explain my plight to the conductor, who ushered me aboard as if their very honor depended on it. I felt sublimely confident, too confident as it turned out.

Maybe a half hour later, traveling the European Road, in essence an interstate highway, I noted that we had passed the exit to Thermopylae. I stood then, a worried look. The conductor seemed to jerk to attention, hurried forward and spoke in rapid-fire Greek to the driver. The next was a squealing of brakes as the bus pulled onto the shoulder. The conductor ran to me, speaking in hurried if not panicked Greek, "*Blah, blah, blah, blah, blah, blah, blah,*" and as if this weren't enough he added a few more, "*Blah, blah, blah.*"

I got the gist of it: Thermopylae was across the freeway and beyond a plain of scrub. I was to disembark right here and make my way there as best I could. Well, hiking is what I do (although if I'd had a bicycle with me I would have just cycled to Thermopylae), so I scuttled off the bus as ordered, and stood there in the swirling dust as the bus jerked into gear and sped off.

Cars whooshed past, meandering from one side of their lane to the other, a driving trait I have noticed in this country. I couldn't cross the freeway, too much traffic, but ahead about a quarter mile I could make out some kind of overpass. So, still a little dumbfounded and dazed from my sudden ejection, I hopped over the scalding guardrail and headed that way.

It was a drainage not a road, heavily churned by road construction equipment. The soil was powdery like lime, clung and itched to confirm that it was. The overpass was low, so I had to duck and waddle to pass beneath it. I was reminded at once of the "holes" below Interstate 40 in Winslow, Arizona that gave local residents afoot access to the Walmart on the other side. (See *Notes from the Field*: p. 279)

I had to scramble up a churned hill of lime on the other side, came out and saw that a stream, the very run-off from the hot sulfur spring of Thermopylae, separated me from the museum and monument. The water was clear, staining the rocks yellow where it ran, and was too wide to jump across. There was no ford. In truth I wanted nothing more than to sit and soak my feet in that water, but with no shade, and feeling as hot and bleak as Death Valley, I continued on for another quarter mile or so to a road that allowed me to cross over.

From there I gained the museum, took more photos of Leonidas, met a Slovakian girl who spoke good English and was so enthused to be here that it sparkled in her eyes. She asked me, "Where is the stone?"

I was pretty sure she meant the engraved stone described by Herodotus; I was also pretty sure the stone was long gone and told her so. She seemed to deflate, then I suggested we go into the museum and ask. Yes, the stone is long gone, but there is a marble marker on Kolonos Hill to honor the last stand of the 300. When the Slovakian girl learned this she ran off at once, giddy to see it. I followed later, after touring the museum in more depth and buying a few trinkets.

Go tell the Spartans... I have seen so many translations of this ancient verse that I have no idea which is right. Some translations say, *Stranger, inform the Lacedemonians that...obedient to their law they fought and died*, along with other translations, none of which have the same resonance as the simplified, *Go tell the Spartans...* Maybe Tennyson actually wrote this one.

I could call it Last Stand Hill, or David Crockett's Barricade, or Culloden Moor, it had that effect on me. Regardless changes in the topography of this place in 2496 years, it is generally accepted that the surviving Spartans, after Leonidas had been killed, made their final stand here, at Kolonos Hill. It is sobering to occupy that same space.

But time was short. I had a 13:00 bus to catch in Thermopyles for the ride back to Kamena Vourla. I waited in the hot sun, not a blade of shade anywhere, 12:55, 12:58—I began to survey the highway ahead for my bus. 13:00, 13:03—something must be wrong. 13:07...no bus. Somehow I knew this would happen. I marched the half mile back to the museum, said there had been no bus, and what should I do?

Kolonos Hill, Thermopylae (Hot Gates in defile to the left)

"But the bus is at 13:30," the woman said.

I doubted this because the woman at the station had told me 13:00, nevertheless I had only minutes before a 13:30 bus would arrive so thanked the woman—*efharisto*—and took off at a full run, glad I hadn't brought my backpack.

I made it with minutes to spare, dripping, 13:29, 13:30. I craned my neck to see up the highway, casting a lengthening shadow. 13:33, 13:35—no bus. I waited in the sun until 13:45, and when no bus came into view I marched back to the museum, produced Argi the taxi driver's card (whom I had met a couple days earlier and who had gotten me out of a previous scrape), and asked the woman to give him a call. Argi arrived within twenty minutes. I was just finishing off a Spartan beer from the museum cafe, smiled goodbye to the ladies, who smiled sweetly in return, grinned at Argi and bid him get me the hell out of here.

It was actually good to see Argi again. He refused to accept the full fare. I paid him what he would accept, and we shook hands. I gave him my contact information in case he ever made it to the States, then walked directly across the street to a cafe to write this.

A lot hinges on tomorrow's bus rides. I hope everything works out, we'll see. But this I know:

After tomorrow I am about done with buses.

MONDAY, JULY 18, 2016

Eleftherios Venizelos Airport, Athens

What a fiasco. The bus from Kammena Vourla didn't drop me at Terminal B, but at a hot, crowded intersection I know not where in Athens. The driver shrugged his shoulders at my questions. He spoke no English, and my phrase book was too slow for his busy schedule. He rattled away in a cloud of exhaust, stranding me wherever the hell I was.

I couldn't find any clues to my location, no street signs, no passersby who spoke English, and no view of the Acropolis in any direction. I finally gave up, flagged a taxi, and got a long and very expensive ride to the airport.

My flight to Oslo boards soon, and now I am definitely done with buses.

2016

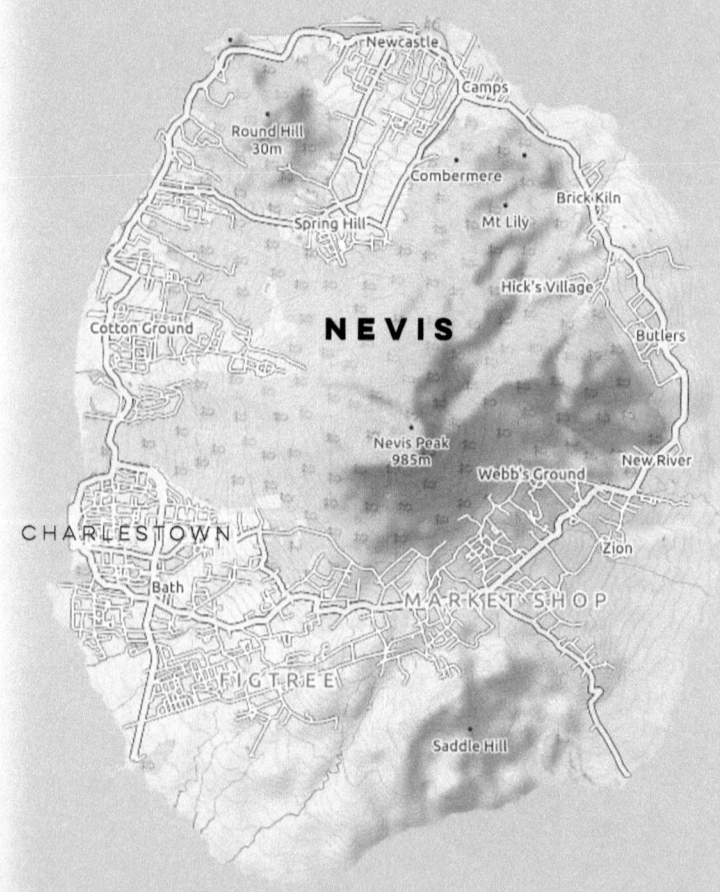

Freshly returned from Europe, and with a new novel churning in my mind, I was soon horrified by obstreperous politics and obdurate neighbors, an impossible environment for creative thought. I called Eloise, my travel agent, and practically begged her to help me escape from the insanity of it all. Her solution was quick, affordable, and richer than I could possibly have anticipated. Less than two weeks after that first phone call, Eloise had me hidden away on the remote island of Nevis in the West Indies, a place so achingly authentic that I changed the setting of my novel, The Latter Half of Inglorious Years, *there from Nashville.*

MONDAY, NOVEMBER 28, 2016

Nevis, West Indies

Arrived St. Kitts late afternoon in the rain. It took a while to get through customs, with plenty of insistent hands out for tips, but the transportation arrangements (requiring several more tips) to get to the island of Nevis were perfect. First a taxi ride along a verdant, humpbacked ridge laced with mist, down to a pier where a water taxi waited, the transfer of luggage and other passengers, and then a bucking and damp crossing to Nevis, which was close enough to be in view, rising deep green from the gray sea, the peak hidden in cloud.

Suzanne and Todd from the real estate company met me on the other side, at a place called Oualie, which has a beach, hotel, pier, bicycle shop, and a bar. I made note of the bicycle shop, which was closed at the time, and the bar, which was open but not on the agenda for the moment. Todd loaded my luggage and bicycle into a sturdy four-wheel drive vehicle, Suzanne got behind the wheel, and we were off as darkness seemed to descend from one moment to the next. As a result, I wasn't able to see much as we drove clockwise around the island on a two-lane road that was rough in places. It began to rain, and then we rounded a rise and I could see stars and gloomy silhouettes of jungle to my right.

We went by two donkeys huddling together off the road. Todd explained that these are all over the island, remnants of a time before the road was built, when Nevisians used them to pull carts. After the road was completed in the 60s, Nevisians bought cars and trucks and set their donkeys loose.

In utter blackness, Suzanne slowed and turned right and then we were climbing at an angle that almost stalled the engine. Suzanne ground the shifter into a lower gear, and with a lurch we climbed and climbed on a rugged narrow track and I held on as if we might careen off the edge of something. Eventually we pulled onto a level spot and stopped. Todd and Suzanne got out with flashlights and led me through a gate to the villa, up some stairs to a veranda, and then through a plank door that opened into a spacious kitchen and living area.

Flipping light switches, they gave me the tour. Two bedrooms upstairs, a bathroom connecting them, wooden shutters on the windows, no screens, a humid breeze, and jungle sounds. The furniture is mostly white wicker with durable blue cushions. I chose the bedroom that opened onto the veranda, dropped my suitcase, thanked Suzanne and Todd, poured a glass of wine, and fell back on a couch in front of a TV tuned to the BBC.

Late, tired and starving, Suzanne had left me a welcome basket that contained the wine, some cheese, crackers, tea and coffee. I drank the wine, ate some cheese and crackers, fended off some mosquitoes, then hauled myself up to get things put away and ready for an extended stay. I showered, figured out how to use the musty mosquito net that draped the bed, and then collapsed into an exhausted sleep.

TUESDAY, NOVEMBER 29, 2016

Nevis, West Indies

My first night in the Caribbean. Slept pretty well, but only from exhaustion. The mosquito net is going to take some getting used to, and the humidity is cloying and constant. Coffee, definitely. More cheese and crackers. I threw open two sets of wide louvered doors to a bright vivid morning, parked my coffee on the veranda rail, and looked down into manicured grounds populated by exotic trees with flowers and fruits I have never seen before, all hemmed in with dense growth that ensures absolute privacy. There's another villa right over there. I can hear some people rustling around, but I can't see them or their villa.

What exactly is a villa, anyway? My dictionary defines it as a large country estate. Okay then, but I think I'll define it as an exotic getaway.

Some monkeys are rustling in the canopy. They are not indigenous, but were brought by Europeans as pets in the seventeenth century. Now, I am told, they are everywhere, and I must take care not to leave the doors open while I am away or leave food unattended on the veranda.

There are hummingbirds, twice the size of the petite ruby-throated hummingbirds back home, and deep purple in color. They are attracted to some red, trumpet shaped flowers in a tall bush just off the veranda, close enough that I could almost reach out and grab them.

Time for a tour in the light of morning.

This villa is called *Southern Comfort*. It's a square, two-story cement structure, white with pale blue trim, a Spanish tile roof, enclosed carport, and tiled, outside stairway. There is a bedroom downstairs withal, a bathroom, and a utility room with washer, water pump and filters. Water comes from a rain cistern under the villa, fed by rain gutters around the roof. Laundry is dried on a clothesline pulley system upstairs. There's much more room here than I will ever need, but the price was right. I'll keep the downstairs bedroom closed off, heavy wood storm shutters latched and locked. The same with the extra bedroom upstairs. I'm not expecting company.

A line of ants is coming up an outside wall, across the veranda, through the kitchen, up onto the countertop, and into the welcome basket that Suzanne left for me. Geez. I swept them out, wiped them off the countertop, and shook them out of the basket and into the sink. I don't think I'll be eating any more of those crackers. Glad I put the rest of the cheese in the fridge. There's some bug spray under the sink, but I don't want to use that stuff if I can help it.

Time to build the bike, the same Cannondale CAADX that I rode in Norway in 2014. I figured I needed a rugged bike for my extended

Southern Comfort

stay here, and after those rough patches during last night's drive, I know I've made the right choice. It didn't take long to get the bike unboxed and assembled. I'm still weary from the serpentine journey to get here, but I've got to go out and find some food. Suzanne wanted me to rent a car, but I said heck no, I'll ride my bike instead. The island is only twenty miles around, after all. That's nothing. There's supposed to be a grocery store a few miles from here called Best Buy, in an area called Gingerland. The next closest store is farther around the island in Charlestown, so Best Buy it is.

Later—

I got into my cycling clothes and helmet, threw on a backpack, carried the CAADX downstairs, and walked it through the gate. A wire fence goes all the way around the place—to keep out voracious donkeys and sheep, I'm told—but much of the fence is lost in thick growths of bamboo and other stuff I can't identify. It was past noon, and man it was hot. Steamy, too. I was sweating just standing there, sweating even more as, in the light of day, I could see for the first time just how steep the road really is. That's if you can call it a road. It looks more like a track through the jungle, two cracked cement strips with tropical plants growing between them, not any kind of grass, but rugged, thorny-looking things that are only cropped when vehicles come and go.

I was on the brakes all the way down, dodging cracks and craters in the narrow cement track that I chose to use as my path. I shot past a couple of houses, not villas because these were the homes of local residents, lots of cement and corrugated metal. Chickens scattered. Scraggly-looking sheep or goats (can't tell for sure which) bungled out of my way. At last I got to the bottom, where my road intersects the main road. There are no street signs, mail boxes or anything like that. I paused to take a look around before I went on because I could easily miss my road on the way back and would then be lost. The best landmark I've got is that my road is the last one before a super steep down-grade to my left, while the road to my right (continuing clockwise) is relatively level. So on the way back, if I find myself suddenly shooting down toward the windward coast at 50 mph I'll know that I missed my turn.

The St. Kitts and Nevis Federation is a former British possession, so they drive on the left, like London, which terrified me when I cycled there in 2011. There wasn't much traffic here, though, so I pushed across into the left lane and hoped for the best.

There were some rolling climbs on the way to Best Buy, enough to have me dripping sweat by the time I found the place. I locked the CAADX to a rail out front while people stared and snickered. I'd hoped to cool off before I went in, but the sweat kept coming and people kept staring, so I gave it up, went in, and was hit by a blast of cold air from an air-conditioning vent aimed right at the door. Oh, man, what a relief. I lingered there for a few minutes, clumsily dodging left and right in the shallow entrance as people went in and out.

Finally composed, although still sopping wet, I took a basket and walked the narrow aisles. Best Buy is not a big place but it has most everything you would expect: meats, produce, canned goods, and an impressive assortment of wine, beer, and liquor. The products are mostly the same as back home, the same brand names. Prices are in ECD—East Caribbean dollars—worth about .37¢ U.S. You can also pay with U.S. dollars and they will do the conversion at the register. In the crush of the checkout line, though, it's hard to tell what conversion rate they're using, so my next ride is already planned: I need to find a bank and draw some ECD. Banks, I assume, will have the best exchange rate.

With my backpack completely stuffed and way too heavy, I got on my bike, started out in the wrong lane, got honked at, crossed over—embarrassed—and started the journey back. I passed a school that had just let out, dozens and dozens of kids in brown and yellow uniforms crossing the road like a tide, waiting on buses (which are elaborately painted minivans) or else filing down narrow tracks that looked more like alleys, passing a few visible homes before disappearing into the lush growth.

Once beyond the kids, I picked up some speed, topped a hill, shot down the other side, and then started another climb. The road undulates on this southeast side of the island, rounding the flank of Nevis Peak, a dormant volcano. Clouds would occasionally part and I could see the peak up and to my left, completely enclosed in foliage, and sometimes to my right I could see over the growth and down to the coast, where waves crashed silently against a rocky shore.

I did shoot past my road, which looks like a driveway to someone's house coming from this direction. Suddenly I was rocketing down a grade, putting on so much speed that I was at the bottom and around a bend before I could stop and turn around. Down there I caught a different view, a coastal plain, an auto race track, of all things, although there were no cars on it then, only sheep and goats, both or the same, couldn't tell.

I was drizzling sweat as I turned around and began the return climb, up off the saddle until my heart felt as if it would explode, and then I had to get off and push. Humiliating. It took a while to get back onto level pavement, where I saddled up with relief. A few pedal strokes and I found my road, which seemed obvious now. I turned onto my road, dug in for the climb, made it about twenty feet and that was it. Too steep to pedal, I wouldn't have been able to climb that grade with a mountain bike! I got off and pushed, and pushed, and pushed, so steep that I was leaning into it, pausing to catch my breath, leaving sweat puddles on the cement. People stared. Monkeys stared. The sheep/goat things stared.

How long did this go on? I didn't time it, but it felt like half an hour. I got to the gate where the pavement finally levelled, rolled through, lifted the bike with the last of my strength and carried it up the stairs to the veranda, where I parked it, dropped pack, stripped naked, and went straight for a cold shower.

Later—

Put away the groceries then spent an hour or more cleaning the bike, which had sweat salt gunked up in everything. I wrung out my clothes, soaked them in the kitchen sink, wrung them out again, then put them on the clothes line to dry. Suddenly it is pitch black yet only 6:00 p.m. Where did the day go? And what's up with all these mosquitoes?

Lights out. I'm going to bed.

WEDNESDAY, NOVEMBER 30, 2016

Southern Comfort

Slept better. This time I tucked the mosquito net all the way around the mattress, so it stood above me in the shape of a tent instead of draping my face like gauze. It started getting light between 5:30 and 6:00 a.m., fully light by 6:30 a.m., and what a sunrise! Morning light comes in through the louvers, shadowed stripes rising across my eyes, better than any alarm clock. I have a view above the canopy to the southeast, a cobalt sea and sunlit cumulus on the horizon, rays streaking down like a painting.

The time zone here is Atlantic Standard Time, which is one hour earlier than Eastern Time. St. Kitts and Nevis doesn't observe Daylight Savings Time, though, so during DST Atlantic Time and Eastern Time are the same. At least I think. Anyway, home is two hours earlier right now.

I didn't leave the villa today. I took it easy instead, still getting used to the place. Did some reading and research for the new novel. Suzanne dropped by to give me a local cell phone and a couple of fans, as much to keep me cool as to—hopefully—blow some of these mosquitoes away.

I think mosquitoes are going to be a problem.

THURSDAY, DECEMBER 1, 2016

Southern Comfort

Slept my best yet! Watched the sun come up then sat down to write the opening to the new novel. Unfortunately it didn't come together for me. Always frustrating.

I cycled down to Best Buy to pick up a few things, came back sopping wet and wiped out just like the day before yesterday. I talked to some people at one of the houses on the way down, and learned that we are in the St. James Windward Parish, in an area called Webbs' Ground. Apparently the main road through here is called Zion.

SATURDAY, DECEMBER 3, 2016

Southern Comfort

I did my first circumnavigation of the island today. I didn't start out with that in mind. Instead, I sat in front of the computer for an hour this morning trying to come up with an opening line, and when nothing came I got up in disgust and rearranged all the furniture in the villa. The place just didn't feel comfortable, but now it does, with couch, chairs and tables in more balanced locations. I positioned my writing desk so that I have a view of the sea to my right and a view of a colorful garden to my left. Too much of either one would be a distraction from my work, too easy for my eyes to wander and then my mind. I need to focus and make words happen. Sure I'll be here for a few months, but months can evaporate if they're not used well.

Afterward, I got ambitious and decided to do all the laundry. The bedsheets are permanently damp from the humidity, and not too comfortable now that I've been sleeping in them for a few nights. So I stripped the bed, found a few other sets of dank sheets on various shelves, carried them all downstairs and threw them in the washer.

I sat on the veranda and sipped a local beer called Carib while the sheets churned below. There are people who can while away the hours just staring out at the ocean, but I'm not one of them. Gotta keep moving; gotta keep doing. I went down to check on the sheets. It's an old washer, really old, rusty in places, creaks and thunks, and as slow as a Model T. Hmm...okay, I needed resupply on food and sundries so I decided to suit up and cycle on down to Best Buy while the washer cycled round and round.

It was about noon by then, as hot and steamy as a laundromat in Louisiana. Best Buy didn't have shaving cream, which I needed, along with a few other odds and ends, so on a whim I pushed on to Charlestown, only five miles away or thereabouts, to see if the IGA had what I needed.

It is a long, winding descent down to Charlestown, beginning just beyond Best Buy and continuing all the way to town. Man, I flew, just hanging on in places. The road levels off at the edge of town, becomes dry and dusty, lots of cars, fewer mufflers. Along the way I caught views of the peak in and out of the clouds, of the sea sprinkled with boats, of chickens and sheep and cement houses, blue, pink, yellow, white, some being taken back by the jungle.

The IGA had what I needed. I tossed the things into my backpack and, since I was down there already and with a helluva climb to get back, carried on into Charlestown to see the place for the first time.

Charlestown looked to me like a miniature New Orleans, narrow sidewalks crowded with locals and a few tourists, some wind-weathered buildings with second floor balconies, people hawking things in the street. The modern buildings were the banks and some government offices. The road curved around along a seawall, boats bobbing, bare masts drumming on the wind. The road curved some more, past the flamingo-colored cement walls of a former resort, like something out of the 1950s. The place looked to be closed down, maybe some squatters in there, hard to tell.

Traffic thinned, a strong tailwind was pushing me along, so I went with it, stomach growling now because I hadn't eaten lunch yet. A sign pointed toward a road to my left, a bar and burger joint down there, the Double Deuce, so I made the quick left, pedaled a quarter of a mile, parked the bike out front and went in.

The Double Deuce is just off the beach, corrugated roof, open to the air on three sides, with wood-plank floor and tables, bar in the back, nets, nautical notions, and international flags for decor. There was only one other person in the place, a big white guy with a British accent. I picked a table with a good breeze, sat back—trying not to drip on the table—and waited. Over my shoulder and beyond the rail, a shirtless guy walked by carrying a big fish by the gills. He went around the corner, maybe toward the kitchen. Fresh catch, I supposed.

I wasn't sitting long before a pretty and poised black woman of indeterminate age appeared with cutlery and a menu. She could have been in her mid-30s if that. Anything older would mean that she had great genes or else there was an actual fountain of youth hidden on the island somewhere. She asked me how I was. I said fine and ordered a Carib, then perused the menu, settled on a burger and fries, and ordered these when she returned. She whisked away with my order, but was back moments later with condiments and such. She arranged these perfectly on my table, little porcelain dishes with little silver spoons in them. She paused, looked things over, then bent down to readjust the spoons so that they leaned at the same angle, flashed me a bright smile, and then she was gone again.

I sipped my beer...no, really I knocked it back like a tall drink of water then looked around for another one. The woman was laughing with the British guy. She saw me, seemed to intuitively know, and was at my table moments later with another Carib. I thanked her, and then she was gone, and then she was back with my burger and fries.

She hovered. Under her gaze, I took an uncertain bite of the burger. She asked me if it was good. Hell, yeah! I replied, and it really was.

I thought about ordering another one since I would probably burn the calories off on the climb back. She sat and watched me eat, and I learned that her name is Shelisa. She spoke with an island accent but not too heavily inflected, although from time to time she would slip into a patois that I couldn't follow, the same way I can bring on an unintelligible Southern accent when I'm not thinking about it.

Finally, full of food and beer, I paid up and made my way back to the bike. At the main road, I went left (clockwise) instead of right (counterclockwise, back the way I came). I figured the distance would be about the same either way, and now I would be able to see the part of the island I missed in the dark the other night. Also, I wasn't prepared to make that big climb up to Gingerland until I had sweated out some of those beers.

The character of the island changed quickly as I went, local housing giving way to resorts and upscale villas. I saw a fruit stand and pulled in, bought some avocados that were as big as softballs. The locals call them "pears," but in their island accent it sounded like

Double Deuce

"peers." Continuing on, noticeably rounding as I went, I came to Oualie Beach, where my water taxi brought me in a few nights ago. There's a resort, a restaurant, the bicycle shop and the short pier I had disembarked on, chairs and umbrellas set up in the sand. St. Kitts is just a healthy swim across the way. The bike shop is small, more of a rental outlet, but I was able to buy a couple of spare tubes. Always need those.

The island changes again past Oualie, becoming arid and dusty in the rain shadow of Nevis Peak. There's cactus and scrubby trees, like south Texas. Signs warned of monkeys crossing, but I didn't see any. I went by a small airport shoved up against the coast, then pedaled into a gusting headwind. The windsock at the airport stood straight out like a pennant. Then new construction, or actually old new construction, a large cement complex, unfinished, starkly gray in the sun, weeds growing through cracks. It didn't look as if anybody had worked on it in years. It looked abandoned.

Onward, a slight climb inland, still rounding, I pedaled past an old Anglican church that looked as if it belonged to the eighteenth century, and then into a pretty little village called Brick Kiln. Kids were off-loading from a bus, crisp school uniforms, books under their arms. I waited for them to scatter across the road then continued on.

Soon I was rounding a sparsely populated coast, climbing gradually, fenced farm plots, a pair of curious donkeys, and then the race track. I groaned because now I had to climb, and I couldn't do it, so I was off the bike and pushing once more while people on porches looked at me as if I had green skin. I made it to the top, breathing hard, my quads trembling, found my road, and then got off to push some more.

Arriving at the villa at last, I left the bike downstairs, too tired to carry it up. Stripping again and leaving my dripping clothes outside on the veranda, I went for a cold shower and then to lie down. The sun was still high in the sky—this whole adventure didn't take two hours although it felt like a full day—but I lay practically comatose until sunset, when I roused myself and brought the bike up. It's too late to dry the sheets, so I'll be sleeping on a bare mattress tonight.

My circumnavigation barely covered twenty miles, but felt like a century ride. Nevis is a small island, but it is so diverse that it feels vast. That butt-kicking climb up the road to the villa is only .32 of a mile, but could as well be 1.32 miles considering how it feels. But now I've done it, and I'm tired, and I'm going to bed.

MONDAY, DECEMBER 5, 2016

Southern Comfort

Didn't sleep well due to things going bump in the night. One of the storm doors had come loose, thumping the wall in the wind, and something got under the mosquito net with me, probably a lizard.

I circumnavigated the island again, this time counterclockwise. I had to get off and push a couple of times during the climb up to Gingerland. Another twenty grueling but enjoyable miles, and I must note, not a single close call with a car.

I found some local coconut rum at Best Buy that I really like. The evening is cool, colors are vivid. A troop of monkeys just went by down there, scratching and exploring and pretending not to notice me.

It would be too easy to go native here.

WEDNESDAY, DECEMBER 7, 2016

Southern Comfort

Windy, windy, windy all night, a constant rush like a storm coming in, settling down when the sun came up, becoming clear and brilliant and I didn't sleep well at all.

I went for another counterclockwise ride, adding five miles as I picked my way through what felt like an endless countryside while looking for a way around that hellish climb up to Gingerland. There isn't one. I wound up on a rutted dirt track with the donkeys, under scrubby trees that blocked the view, well below Gingerland and totally lost. You wouldn't think that would be possible on such a small island. I went by some corrugated shacks but saw no one. It felt eerie, as if people were watching me through gaps in the walls, as if I had bumbled into an area where strangers shouldn't go, like taking the wrong exit off the interstate in eastern Tennessee, trying to get back around, following the road until it narrows and narrows and the next thing you know you're in some sickly woods where stills and marijuana patches are tended by people you only ever see in horror movies. It occurred to me that if I were to be waylaid on the island it would happen here, and if it did happen I would never be found. I would become a disappearance, a mystery they might write books about one day.

Enough of this, I followed a rutted track inland, a trail really, knowing that sooner or later the terrain would begin to rise and I might intersect with a track or road in one of the neighborhoods below Gingerland. After a short time that felt like a long time, I came to a sandy cement road that seemed to draw a straight line between the coast to my right and the heights to my left. Curious, I went right, following the road until it seemed to fade into sand about two hundred feet from a pretty beach. I saw some people walking on the beach, locals, not tourists, and a couple of nice beach houses, feeling completely remote even though Best Buy couldn't be more than two miles away.

I turned around and pedaled for as long as I could, finally got off and pushed, went through some shaded neighborhoods, got back on and pedaled against the incline, huffing and huffing, my heart about to explode. A boy came up beside me on his BMX bike, too big for the bike, all knees and pointy elbows and with a bright white grin. He popped a wheelie and stayed with me as I wished for just one more gear. Finally I laughed—I had to laugh. The kid was great. I wished I still had his resilience.

Shortly I came onto the main road, called Beach Road through that area, turned right, stopped in at Best Buy as a matter of routine (when you're on a bike on a volcanic island, never pass a store without stopping to get something), and then continued on to the villa, .32 of a mile that felt as if I were climbing with anchors chained to me.

Back at the villa, another routine: stripping on the veranda, sopping clothes on the rail, cold shower and a beer to match.

What an adventure in just twenty-five miles.

THURSDAY, DECEMBER 8, 2016

Southern Comfort

Another windy night, and a gray day but no rain.

At last, fashioned some opening paragraphs that I'm happy with. Now I can dig in and get my word count up.

My quads are still sore from yesterday, so I left the bike at the villa and went for a hike instead, more of an exploration, really. The jungle is thick, finally too thick to get through. Vines hang like baleen from the canopy, ready to sift and tangle and ingest you like a verdant whale. I am told there are no snakes here, no jungle predators beyond the microscopic, so beating through the bush is safe as far as that goes. There is a poisonous tree called the manchineel, so poisonous that the locals speak of it in hushed tones. The fruit, which look like little green apples, are deceptively sweet and decidedly dangerous. They have been called "little apples of death." The sap causes acid-like burns. People who have unwittingly taken shelter under the manchineel tree during the rain have been badly burned. I should be okay, though, since the tree doesn't grow at this elevation, but only along the coast.

Supposedly there is a trail from here up to the peak, but I couldn't find it. Instead I would emerge from the bush onto another of the unnamed cement tracks like the one leading to my villa. They seem to crisscross the jungle invisibly, unmapped and unknown except to those whose villas are secreted up here. Occasionally I would come across an old stone foundation, moss-covered stones held in place by creeping roots, and unrecognizable rusting iron artifacts, leftovers from an earlier century.

Following the winding cement tracks, I did get turned around and lost. I could hear a bulldozer back in the bush, doubtless scraping

Nevis Jungle

away at a foundation for a new villa. I tried to move toward it, to ask directions, but no winding track I followed ever went there. With no view through the canopy, I used the faint warmth of a shrouded sun as a guide, and eventually came out on the road to my villa, but well below. I sighed, turned left and climbed, and when I got to my villa I popped the cap on a cold Carib, took a long swallow, propped myself against the veranda rail and marveled at the jungle that completely enclosed my view. I probably didn't hike more than a mile, although I could have gone ten for all the jungle would tell me. So much experience in such a small place. Amazing.

John Glenn died today, aged 95. They are all gone now.

SATURDAY, DECEMBER 10, 2016

Southern Comfort

Finished the opening scene today, all while swatting mosquitoes. They are so bad that I took the mosquito net from the spare bedroom and tried to find a way to hang it over my writing desk. This worked after a fashion, but it got too hot under the net, and I couldn't stand the way it kept catching on my elbows. I can't work like this, so I called Suzanne. They're going to see about installing some screens for me.

SUNDAY, DECEMBER 11, 2016

Southern Comfort

Very windy all night, the mosquito net wafting and the shutters rattling. Makes you appreciate the quiet of an air-conditioned space. The things we take for granted...

Went for a counterclockwise ride with a stop at the Double Deuce for lunch. I lucked into their Yorkshire Pudding Sunday. Normally you have to make a reservation for this, but they had a couple left over so I scored one. It was very good.

I went off route twice trying to find a way down to the coastline that I can see from the villa. I did finally get down there, but only along a washed out road and then overland across a sloping plain of desiccated grass, parting donkeys as I went. This is the windward side of the island, so the coast is rocky and full of detritus and litter. Plus the surf is rough, not a place you would want to swim. I did come across an eighteenth-century sugar plantation, which is being restored as an historical site and tourist draw. The cauldrons are still there for boiling and refining the sugar, very big, very old, and very rusty, but thick enough to rust for centuries and still be usable. The stone buildings were actually in pretty good shape. The place looked as if you could just about get it up and running today. Of course it ran on slave labor, and was abandoned along with slavery in the nineteenth century.

TUESDAY, DECEMBER 13, 2016

Southern Comfort

It rained hard on and off all night, a sluicing, tropical rain that flashed through the gutters and into the cistern. I could hear the cavernous tinkling of water somewhere deep below. There is a gauge attached to the wall behind the couch, a piece of wood like a heavy yardstick, ruled in centimeters and coming up through a small hole in the floor. I had wondered what this was, now it's obvious, and it has risen significantly since yesterday. I guess I don't have to worry about running out of water for a while.

The wind that came along with this rain was ferocious, a big blow, which had me up in the night to close all of the storm shutters. I slept well after that, the villa buffeted but weather-tight, nevertheless I woke up this morning with a cold, a real cold, sore throat, feverish, &c. Now where did this come from?

Despite my cold, I did some good work on the novel this morning, which dawned sunny as if last night's storm were only an illusion. A man named Rupesh came in the afternoon to install some ingenious screens over the door and window louvers. He also screened off a section of the veranda, so now I'll get some relief from these incessant mosquitoes.

Man, I feel like hell. No rum on the veranda this evening, I'm going to bed.

WEDNESDAY, DECEMBER 14, 2016

Southern Comfort

It's not a cold, it's the full-blown flu! I haven't had the flu in decades. There must be a bug down here that I've never been exposed to before.

I soaked my sheets through last night, and now the fever is back. I feel woozy, cold...I feel bad and I don't have anything here to treat this with, not even aspirin, and I sure as hell don't have the strength to cycle to Best Buy.

Later—

I called a taxi to take me down to Ram's Supermarket in Charlestown. I had him take me there because it's the only place that has an ATM that dispenses U.S. dollars as well as East Caribbean dollars, and I needed cash so that I could pay for the taxi. The taxi was a plain black minivan, not elaborately painted like many of the others, or maybe it's the buses that are painted, you can tell which are which by the license plates but I don't have the energy to think about it right now.

The taxi was $40 USD plus tip (ouch), but he showed up right on time to take me back to the villa. I was so feverish on the return trip that I just wanted to wilt into his comfy velvet seats and stay in that heavenly cool blast from his air-conditioner.

I bought cough syrup, ibuprofen, corn tortillas, chicken soup, and hot peppers (they didn't have Tabasco). Whenever I'm sick like this I make what I call Tabasco Soup, which is shredded corn tortillas in chicken soup, and with enough Tabasco to turn it pink. I know it sounds horrible, but it will clear your sinuses in an instant, and I get a surge of energy from it. Anyway, it works for me whenever I'm not feeling well. I've been making it for years.

THURSDAY, DECEMBER 15, 2016

Southern Comfort

My fever broke overnight. I soaked the sheets again but I do feel somewhat better.

SATURDAY, DECEMBER 17, 2016

Southern Comfort

A strange, blustery day, with rain followed by sun followed by rain followed by sun. I feel better but lethargic, not even enough energy to write. I'm glad I brought plenty of books.

MONDAY, DECEMBER 19, 2016

Southern Comfort

Feeling much better, and slept pretty well last night, especially now that I've figured out which doors and shutters are banging in the wind. Tightened a few screws here and there, padded one shutter with a towel, and now the night sounds are comforting, like a night in shelter on the Appalachian Trail.

It rained heavily in bursts throughout the night, and continued through the morning and afternoon, although it became gorgeous near sunset.

I needed more supplies but couldn't get out on the bicycle because of the weather. I guess this bicycle idea just isn't going to work out. Maybe if it weren't for the big climbs...Anyway, I don't want to rent a car, I really don't. Maybe I can rent a scooter. That would work, wouldn't it? Why not?

TUESDAY, DECEMBER 20, 2016

Southern Comfort

It was blustery last night, but I slept through it and slept quite well. I've been here three weeks, and that's how long it has taken to get the hang of this place, to get the environment just right, to track down all the bumps and bangs, to get the mosquitoes under control, and to figure out how to handle the ants.

The ants...

...they found the smallest gap in the seal around the refrigerator door, which I opened yesterday morning to find hundreds of their cooling carcasses on every shelf. Persistent little buggers, their marching line came down the side of the fridge, across the floor, out the door, across the veranda, and down the outside wall. It reminds me of that story we read in junior high school, *Leiningen Versus the Ants*, except that these ants don't seem to be interested in stinging me, they're just a nuisance. On top of that—and I don't get this at all—they even climbed into the filtered-water pitcher that I keep on the kitchen counter, which I didn't notice until I had swallowed a few of them. Gack!

So I cleaned out the fridge, made sure the door closed securely, swept the line of ants over the edge of the veranda, then wiped down the floor and counters with cleaner. Now I keep all food items—especially the sugar—in the fridge, and I have parked my water pitcher in a basin of water as a barrier to keep the ants out. I was gratified this morning to find that my efforts had worked: no ants anywhere in the kitchen, and I was able to solve the problem without using bug spray.

On to today:

I did some good work on Chapter Two, then went for a clockwise ride with a segue to the Double Deuce for a cold Carib. Shelisa told me about a guy named Kevin who rents scooters, so I'm going to give him a call.

WEDNESDAY, DECEMBER 21, 2016

Golden Rock Inn

On and off rain all night, but sunny in the morning. I didn't feel like writing or cycling, so I followed a rumor that I could get to a high-end restaurant and hotel called Golden Rock Inn via a trail at the top of my road. Using a broomstick as a hiking pole, I poked and explored the upper end of my road, where it is swallowed by the bush, found a faint trace and followed it.

Ducking below limbs, stepping over moss-covered logs, and pushing my way through hanging vines, I crossed above a deep gorge, green and slick with volcanic rock, following instinct more than a trail, leaving blazes so that I could find my way back.

I encountered more hidden jungle roads, built cairns where I crossed, entered a clearing, like an Appalachian bald, that gave an extraordinary view of the dense canopy below and eventually the sea. I knew that the main road was down there, and numerous houses, but they were completely enshrouded by the dense jungle. I could as well have been the only person on a deserted island as far as I could tell from that spot.

I emerged onto another road, the ubiquitous cement strips, but better maintained, shaded under the canopy like a pretty garden path. Something told me to turn right on the road, up a grade that had me puffing, and then the road leveled, an immaculate hedge materialized out of the jungle, a few more feet to a gate, and there was the sign: Golden Rock Inn.

The grounds are a lovely garden, grass mown close like soft green velvet. I wandered through this, found wide steps in an aged stone wall, and took these up to a sunny open area arranged with tables and stone pergolas and a water garden. It was about noon. A few people were seated for lunch, so I claimed a table in a shaded breezeway and waited.

My waitress soon arrived with a menu. I ordered a Guinness to assuage my jungle thirst while I perused the menu. The bottle sweated in the humidity and tasted perfect. I eventually ordered the catch of the day, dolphin fish, which is not the mammal dolphin, but a fish sometimes called mahi-mahi or dorado. I also ordered conch soup (my first since Key West eight years ago), salad, and another beer.

The atmosphere of this place is great, the food equally so; the breeze is cool and they have free Wi-Fi. I think I'll order another Guinness and hang out for a while.

THURSDAY, DECEMBER 22, 2016

Southern Comfort

Gray and wet this morning, so I stayed in and did some solid work on Chapter Two.

I got my scooter today, but Kevin didn't come by to pick me up until 5:00 p.m. We drove to the other side of the island to get the scooter, in the area of the airport, which is almost directly across the island from here. Sure it's a small island, but that distance grows longer every time I cycle it.

Kevin provided me with a helmet, and then spent time making sure I understood the controls and could handle the thing. He told me stories of tourists who wouldn't listen to him, and would crash his scooters moments after renting them...and then demand a refund! What dicks, I said. I rode motorcycles for years, but it's been years since those years happened, so I paid attention to what Kevin was saying, about leaning and braking and keeping my feet on the floorboards. Don't stick your foot out, he said, you'll lose balance. This is a scooter, not a motorcycle. Kevin's articulation is so precise that it's actually a feature of his personality. You notice it right away.

I started getting worried, though, when his instruction ventured into the sunset. The dark of night comes from one moment to the next here, and I don't see well at night anymore. Couple that with an unfamiliar scooter and feral donkeys, and I wondered if I would make the ten miles back to the villa before morning.

Kevin shook my hand and sent me on my cautious way as the last of the day noticeably curtained down. I proceeded in the dark—and it was really dark—feeling cocooned in tangible night, like that drive I made to El Paso back in the 70s, or my night-hike out of Blackrock Hut during my 2008 Appalachian Trail hike.

I kept my eyes on the road, no painted stripes or anything else to mark the borders, just asphalt slightly brighter than the night, some climbs and dips, a pair of donkeys that came out of the dark at the last moment, but on the side of the road, and then I could see a third donkey down, definitely dead, its companions lingering, perhaps mourning. Someone must have blown through here not too far ahead of me, taken out the donkey and kept on going. The speed limit out here, in what the people at the Double Deuce call "the country," is 40 mph, but cars—and especially dump trucks—have passed me going much faster than that while I was cycling.

I slowed to 20 mph and willed my pupils to dilate farther.

Soon—although it seemed like a long, long time—I was on the steep climb through Zion, which I made without incident, but then I came to my road and the real challenge of this ride.

I had to choose a cement strip, the one to the left or the one to the right. Both had cracks and broken sections, one as narrow as the other, so I took the one to the right, hoping I would be more familiar with it.

I did make it about halfway before the engine began to bog down from the grade and the strain. The scooter is an automatic, no clutch to pop, so I gunned it and gunned it and hoped for the best because there was no way I could push that heavy scooter up a hill that steep.

I was going too slow, beginning to wobble, so I did what? I stuck out my foot, against all of Kevin's advice, and I fell right over into the sticky bushes in the pitch black and even slid back a foot or so.

Oh, man, what a fiasco. I was scratched, but more embarrassed than hurt. At least there were no witnesses, too dark for that, although I had a feeling that the people who lived not far below where I crashed had probably heard the whole thing and were snickering at the predicament the new resident tourist had gotten himself into.

After a few calming breaths, I squeezed the brake and got the scooter back on two wheels. Then I got it started and, with middle finger still squeezing the brake, twisted the throttle with my palm, getting the revs up, and then I let the brake go, the scooter lurched, and I jumped aboard, hanging on like a cowboy who has slipped off the back of his saddle.

It was an ungainly, tank-slapping climb, but I made it without falling again, and I don't think I did any damage to the scooter. In the morning I'm going to have to go up and down that climb until I can get it right.

SATURDAY, DECEMBER 24, 2016

Southern Comfort

A lot of rain overnight, and a heavy sky this morning. I set out on a counterclockwise ride at about 11:30 a.m., cycled through some rain, but then it cleared out to become hot and humid.

I stopped in at Oualie and finally met Winston, the owner of Cycle World. He is about my age, super fit, looks a lot like Idris Elba, and speaks with an energetic English accent. I described my rides to him and he laughed. It is a volcanic island, he said, but he can make both those big climbs without any problem. The steep climb through Zion is called the Killer Bee, he told me. Whenever elite cyclists come to the island, he takes them up that climb. This stimulated me into making it a goal to do both climbs without having to get off. Just focus and breathe, I thought. Keep the heart rate down and you can do it.

Winston and I promised to get together soon for a ride, and then I continued on to the Double Deuce, where I had a burger and one too many beers, which just about toppled me off the bike going up the climb to Gingerland. I had to get off and push, and the goal I set at Cycle World seemed to have happened weeks ago.

New goal: one beer only at the Double Deuce when I'm on the bicycle.

SUNDAY, DECEMBER 25, 2016

Southern Comfort

Christmas Day, a brilliant morning and not too hot. Worked on Chapter Two, then took the scooter out to do some exploring. I love going around the island on Sundays because the churches are full and I can hear people singing. I think there are more churches on this island than in the entirety of Nashville, and just about every denomination you can name; and this with a population of only eleven thousand or thereabouts. Nevisians are religious people. There is a church in Charlestown—I didn't catch the denomination—open to the air, and the singing is so loud and vibrant that I like to park in the shade just to listen. I could go in, I guess, but I think I enjoy it more from outside.

The people down in Zion erected a Christmas tree on a bluff overlooking the sea, with "Seasons Greetings" spelled in red tinsel, and lots of colorful lights. I've been down to see it at night, and think it is as pretty as any Christmas display I've seen at home, maybe more so since it is juxtaposed against the sea.

I also found some hidden beaches today that I think I'll visit again, including a black-sand beach near the airport.

After a few enjoyable hours on the scooter, I treated myself to a

Christmas dinner at Yachtsman Grill on Montpelier Beach. It's an expat hangout, but most everything else, including the Double Deuce, was closed. Still, good food, good beer, and a good view—all in all, a good Christmas.

TUESDAY, DECEMBER 27, 2016

Southern Comfort

I started Chapter Three and made good progress, then went out and blazed a proper trail to Golden Rock, where I had lunch. Later, a guy named Bee Man came for a visit.

"Inside," he hollered from the base of the stairs.

"Hello," I hollered back.

A scruffy guy, perhaps my age or less, came up the stairs and had a seat. Suzanne had told me about Bee Man, who really is a bee man. His real name is Quentin, he's an expat from England, and he came to the island years ago under the auspices of the government to cultivate bees to aid the island's agriculture. This went on for some years before his funding was pulled. Nowadays he does odd jobs so that he can stay on the island.

This was all very interesting, but the main reason he came to see me is because he has also hiked the Appalachian Trail. He didn't finish, he said, because his visa expired before he could, but he does hope to get back eventually to complete his hike.

We talked for over two hours. Hollering "Inside," he explained, is how Nevisians announce themselves when they visit someone's home. There are no doorbells, and the way the houses are designed—without internal stairways—people could be upstairs or down and how would you know? So they holler "Inside" to let you know they are there, and you answer them by hollering "Outside" so that they know where you are in the house. What a charming and ingenious local custom.

Bee Man is well known on the island, and often guides hikers up to Nevis Peak for a fee. I'm sure I will see him again.

WEDNESDAY, DECEMBER 28, 2016

Charlestown, Nevis

I've been here for a month already. A month! 25% of the experience is over, and I feel as if I have only just gotten settled in.

A month also means that I have to pay rent on the villa, which I will do in person at Suzanne's office at Cliffdwellers, a high-end expat development a mile clockwise from the ferry port. But first I have to renew my visa at the immigration office, which is where I am now... which is where I have been waiting for the past hour.

It's well past lunch. I rode in on the scooter this morning in order to get a head start on the visa-renewal process, came in, took a seat, was more or less ignored by the receptionist, who held up a halting finger when I took a breath to speak with him. Your turn will come, he said, eyes elsewhere when he said it. I sat for about ten minutes, my eyes wandering around the modern, spacious reception area, to the heavy wood door—closed—with the Nevis governmental seal affixed. Somehow I knew that I wouldn't be seen until that door opened. And then I spotted the sign on white A4 paper, black ink off someone's printer: *Proper Attire Only. No Shorts, T-shirts, Sandals.*

I looked myself over, even though I didn't need to. I was wearing shorts, a T-shirt, and sandals, and was now terribly embarrassed. When you travel to someone else's country, you show respect and obey the rules, and here I was in their government offices breaking their rules. I got up and slinked out, hoping I hadn't been noticed (but of course I was), hopped on the scooter and headed straight back to the villa.

After a shower (because I had gotten slimy on the ride to Charlestown and back), I dressed in jeans, a button-up shirt, proper shoes, then blazed back to Charlestown.

And now I've been waiting an hour while people come and go, not many, though. Bee Man breezed through with a handful of papers he hoped would finally earn him permanent residency. I don't know how that worked out. The door opened for him; he went in; the door closed; the door opened again a short time later, and Bee Man left with a subdued air, never looking my way.

The door has remained closed. No one has been called to go in. It's down to me and an older black guy who hasn't been interested in talking. It's like a competition, me or him—one of us gets to go next and we both know it. It should be me, I was here first, but he looks like a local. Maybe they get priority.

The door opens. We both lean forward expectantly. A professionally poised woman steps out, looks at me and nods. I'm elated, and actually cast a victorious glance at the other guy. I go into her office and sit. She closes the door, comes to her desk, sits, rummages through some papers, holds up a halting finger when I take a breath to speak. She peruses her papers, finally sets them aside, crosses her arms on her desk and looks up.

"What can I do for you?" she asks.

"I need to renew my visa," I answer as patiently and nicely as possible. My fate may rest on this woman's mood. I show her my passport, my thirty-day visa stamp.

"How long are you staying?" she asks.

"Until the end of March," I answer.

"Why are you on Nevis?" she asks.

"I'm writing a novel," I answer.

"Hmm," she ponders. And then she pulls forms from a slotted bin on her desk, one, two, three, four. "Fill these out," she says, "and come back tomorrow."

I am then dismissed.

THURSDAY, DECEMBER 29, 2016

Southern Comfort

I got the visa extension resolved today. It cost me $62.00, and was almost a fiasco because I am supposed to pay in ECD but all I had was twenties in USD. The woman seemed bemused, as if nothing like this had ever happened before, and perhaps it hadn't. The expats at the Cafe des Arts in Charlestown told me that Continentals usually ignore extending their visas, and carry on without ever a problem. My luck runs counter to that, I said. Better not to take chances. At any rate, the woman found a cash box with loose dollar bills and assorted change, and meticulously counted $18.00 back to me in exchange for four twenties. She issued me a visa through April in case I decided to stay longer, so at least I don't have to worry about this anymore.

SATURDAY, DECEMBER 31, 2016

Southern Comfort

It rained overnight and this morning. I thought up a great name for one of my characters while I was sleeping, but didn't get up to write it down and now it's gone.

 It has more or less rained all day, and it's still raining. During a brief lull, I made it to Best Buy for some groceries and a bottle of celebratory rum. There will be New Year's celebrations all over the island, I could pick and choose where to go, but I don't want to get out in this weather. I'll celebrate here with the monkeys.

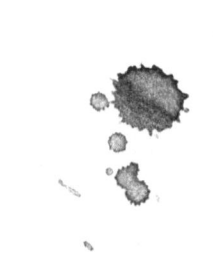

2017

SUNDAY, JANUARY 1, 2017

Nevis, West Indies

My first-ever New Year's Day overseas, and what a great day it was.

I saw fireworks from the veranda last night, bursting high above the canopy. It wasn't a huge show, probably local residents, but plenty of color and moment to go along with my rum.

This morning dawned clear and vivid and reasonably cool. Chapter Three is in the can, so to celebrate I went for a counterclockwise ride. The beauty on these clear days just squeezes your throat—so much diversity, so many colors. And I almost made it to the top at Gingerland without having to get off, just the last little bit.

I'll make it next time.

WEDNESDAY, JANUARY 4, 2017

Double Deuce

Went for a counterclockwise ride and made it over the top at Gingerland without having to walk the bike! First time! And so to celebrate, I'm here at the Double Deuce, talking to Shelisa and Julie and sipping a Guinness or three.

MONDAY, JANUARY 9, 2017

Oualie Beach

Chapter Four is in the can, started on Chapter Five. Took the scooter around to Yachtsman Grill for lunch, and now I'm at Cycle World in Oualie limin' with Winston and looking across both beach and bay at St. Kitts.

Do you know that I came to spend four months on a Caribbean island and didn't bring a swimsuit?

WEDNESDAY, JANUARY 11, 2017

Southern Comfort

Some intense power surges last night. I'm told this happens from time to time because power comes from diesel generators that are not always well attended. The computers seem to be okay, but the refrigerator has been blown, along with a lot of lightbulbs. An electrician came and fixed everything, so now I am back at work on Chapter Five.

THURSDAY, JANUARY 12, 201

Southern Comfort

Worked hard on Chapter Five all day, so hard that I didn't get up, go out, or even stop for lunch. With a bottle of wine and a handful of snacks, I finished the chapter—and then I had to go lie down.

TUESDAY, JANUARY 17, 2017

Southern Comfort

Another rainy and windy night. I thought I might cycle today, but I got caught up in Chapter Six and finished it. I spent the rest of the day doing some needed repairs to the bike. I tightened some spokes and trued the wheels, which take a beating on that really rough stretch of road on the north side near the medical university. I also pulled the front derailleur and cleaned the sweat salt out of it. Now it's shifting much smoother and I'm ready to ride.

THURSDAY, JANUARY 19, 2017

Southern Comfort

Calm and sunny at last, and dry overnight. Stayed in to work on Chapter Seven.

An event occurred tonight that I can only call "The Invasion of the Million Bugs." After sunset, while I was sipping rum and watching the news on BBC, I looked up to notice a swarm of little flying bugs on a lampshade. Soon they were everywhere, smothering every light. Suzanne had those screens installed, but there is still a gap below the doors and that's how they were getting in.

Man, these weren't just a few bugs, this was a mass invasion. They weren't stinging bugs, but there were so many of them that I actually inhaled a few.

I leapt to the bathroom, grabbed towels and shoved them under the doors. This slowed the bugs' progress, but there were already a million of them in the villa. I have truly never experienced anything like this. Even that swarm of mosquitoes I encountered in the Arctic National Wildlife Refuge in the 90s didn't compare to this.

So now I'm going to turn out all the lights, get in bed under the mosquito net, and just ride this thing out.

FRIDAY, JANUARY 20, 2017

Southern Comfort

This morning looked like the aftermath of war. There were dead bugs scattered like black sand under every lamp, and their little bodies were stuck by the thousands in the screens where they were trapped like fish in a gill net. I swept them out, used the broom on the screens, and was able to clear out most of them. Others that were more tenaciously trapped in the screens will go back to nature by and by. I've asked around, and nobody seems to know what these bugs are. At least they didn't return tonight. Maybe it was a one-time migration, or breeding frenzy, or something like that.

Afterward I went for a counterclockwise ride, met up with Winston, and cycled with him as far as Pond Hill in the climb up to Gingerland. He really is a strong cyclist. That climb didn't faze him at all.

Later I took the scooter around to Indian Summer for lunch. They have the best chicken curry I have ever tasted, and plenty of cold Guinness to go with it.

MONDAY, JANUARY 23, 2017

Yubrenta's Snackette

It got so cool last night that I had to throw on a blanket. That's something I didn't expect here. It was nice, though.

Finished Chapter Seven, then took the scooter around to this place for lunch because Winston recommended it. Yubrenta's Snackette is a small, open-air eatery located between Indian Summer and Oualie on the northwest side of the island, so an almost exact diagonal from the villa. I've seen this place on my rides but never thought to stop in because I thought "snackette" meant it was a convenience store of some kind.

The food is local and ethnic and really, really good. I had salt fish, rice and beans, and of course a Guinness. Someone told me I must be the only white guy on the island who drinks Guinness. Well, I like Guinness, and I'm going to order another one and hang out for a while.

THURSDAY, JANUARY 26, 2017

Cycle World, Oualie

The power was out for most of the morning, but I still managed to do some good work on Chapter Eight before my laptop battery began to fade.

Took the scooter down to the Double Deuce for lunch, then met up with Winston here to buy some cycling shorts. I've worn mine out already. How many times have I circumnavigated this island on my bicycle? I've lost count, but obviously enough to wear out my cycling shorts. I'm going to cut the chamois pad out, and then I'll have some nice Spandex swimming shorts.

MONDAY, JANUARY 30, 2017

Southern Comfort

Finished Chapter Eight then went for a counterclockwise ride. Coming here to work really was a great decision.

SATURDAY, FEBRUARY 4, 2017

Indian Summer

I've been stuck on Chapter Nine, but I made a breakthrough today, I think. What a relief. Writer's block is the worst.

So now I'm at Indian Summer to celebrate. Man, this curry is good.

MONDAY, FEBRUARY 6, 2017

Southern Comfort

Heavy rain overnight. I'm not feeling well for some reason.

I spent on the order of $60.00 today to FedEx a T-shirt to my son Jarred for his birthday. So yeah, that was ridiculous, but I wanted him to have a unique gift. The T-shirt is from Indian Summer. It's black and says, "No Worry, Eat Curry," on the front, with a skull on the back. I don't know what the skull means, but I figured Jarred would like it.

Then I had to go to the dentist because one of my fillings came out. The Cuban dentist comes to Charlestown once a week, so there was a line of us waiting when he arrived. We were all handled quickly and politely. The equipment looked as if it were out of the 50s (and perhaps it was), but it was clean and did the job. The dentist spoke a little English, but I mostly just pointed and he took care of it. He was very professional. My bill was—get this—only $30.00! Maybe I'll need some more dental work before I leave. I doubt I'll find it cheaper anywhere.

Oh yeah, this was weird: on the customs form for the T-shirt, I had to list "T-shirt," of course, but I also had to write "100% cotton," and then select "woven" instead of "knit." What's that all about?

WEDNESDAY, FEBRUARY 8, 2017

Southern Comfort

Still not feeling great, but managed to finish Chapter Nine. Took the scooter around to Suzanne's office in Cliffdwellers to pick up some books from Doreen, Suzanne's assistant. Thank goodness they finally arrived. I was getting desperate. Gotta have books.

FRIDAY, FEBRUARY 10, 2017

Cycle World, Oualie

Building bikes with Winston. He just got a shipment in. I forgot how much I enjoy building bikes. It's been—what?—nine years since I left Spring Valley Bikes in Houston. So yeah, this is work to most people, but for me it's fun.

Earlier, I worked on Chapter Ten, then had lunch at the Double Deuce.

SATURDAY, FEBRUARY 11, 2017

Yuhventa's Snackette

I'm eating pig snout soup. Those are five words I would never have expected to write. It's a bit gelatinous, but you know, it tastes pretty damn good.

Finished Chapter Ten this morning.

MONDAY, FEBRUARY 13, 2017

Basseterre, St. Kitts

Basseterre, the capital of St. Kitts, is congested chaos. Even on the scooter I had a hard time finding a place to park, for fear that I would unwittingly leave it in a no-parking zone and find it gone when I got back. Otherwise, every marked parking place and street curb was taken. I wound up leaving the scooter about a half mile away from downtown, at a curb in front of a pink house, and between two other cars parked there. It should be safe enough, I thought, but still I walked away with trepidation. What would happen if I lost the scooter? How would I get back to Nevis? How pissed would Kevin be?

Fortunately, nothing untoward happened to the scooter.

Chapter Ten is in the can, there are now more days behind on Nevis than ahead, and I hadn't been to St. Kitts since I flew in and taxied out some seventy-seven days ago or thereabouts. I made the decision to go to St. Kitts on the spur of the moment, but with still enough time to ask Kevin's permission to take his scooter across The Narrows to the other part of this federation. He consented and off I went.

I made it to the Sea Bridge ferry port, near Suzanne's office, well before the 11:00 a.m. departure, and then waited until 11:30 for the ferry to show up. Nothing as grand as the ferries of Norway, this ferry was more utilitarian but it did the job. I scooted aboard, parked against a bulkhead, strapped the scooter to some wooden stays as instructed, then paid my $50 ECD passage, or roughly $18.50 USD.

The crossing went quick enough, people swim across The Narrows, after all. The ferry dropped its ramp in a little sandy inlet on a bit of cement skirt, with a small, boxy office, some rusting ironwork, and nothing else. They let me off first since I was more mobile, but I pulled over anyway to wait for all the cars to go first, otherwise I would have had them on my tail all the way to Basseterre.

St. Kitts is shaped somewhat like a meat cleaver, with the handle dangling down toward The Narrows. I would have to traverse that handle, some ten to twelve miles, to reach Basseterre, on a two-lane road that undulates along the top of some surprisingly mountainous terrain.

With all the cars gone, I set out at my own pace. I climbed at first—unexpectedly steep—sighing in relief because I recognized right then that I would never have been able to cycle this. That had been my original plan, to bring the CAADX across, spend the day cycling St. Kitts, and then be back on Nevis by sunset for beers at the Double

Nevis Peak

Deuce. I nixed that plan only because I knew I would be able to cover more distance with the scooter and I wanted to see as much as I could. Again I sighed. If I'd come on the bicycle I would have been stuck in that sandy inlet until the 4:00 p.m. ferry.

I came to a wide tunnel through a mountain, galvanized metal, bright concrete, definitely new and undoubtedly expensive to build. St. Kitts has received some largesse from the United Nations, it would seem, as this was the most European-modern-like thing I had seen since Norway. The views before and after the tunnel were expansive, looking back toward the emerald of Nevis and ahead to sharp ridges that held the road high above arcs of beach on either side, as if scalloped into the precipitous cliffs. I stopped for photos, trying to compare this to anything I had seen before, and then I came to the conclusion that I had never seen anything like this before.

Onward, sharp drops between peaks, straining climbs up the other side. This part of the island is in the rain shadow, so the overgrowth is sparse and scrubby, opening the view to crashing waves below and the undulating road ahead. Basseterre was not in view, perhaps some haze ahead but that could as well have been a cloud.

After about eight miles, I left the peninsula and entered the main part of the island. The views had been so expansive, and the short distances so deceptively long, that my mind wanted to call this "the mainland." Habitation began to dot the roadside, and then more. The road went to four lanes, and retail began to intersperse with the homes. There was nothing pretty about this side of town. It was hot and dusty, the buildings worn and faded, and the traffic was picking up. I soon came to a traffic circle, a big one—no worries, I've negotiated these all over Europe—on a ways and then another circle—still no problem—and then I came to a traffic circle that so confounded me that I had to pull over and study the thing. It was two circles together, touching in the middle, with an oval road going around both along with the traditional exits—and this with drivers in the left lanes going clockwise rather than what we would be accustomed to outside of Britain. I—simply—could—not—figure—it—out. There were three and four lanes in there, cars and trucks coming from every which way. The roads were too wide to cross on foot. If I rode into that, I would get hit, I was sure of it.

The road I needed to take to Basseterre was well across the way, in the other circle. I wasn't lost, I could see the sign, I just couldn't figure out how to get there. What a crazy mess. Who thought this monstrosity up, and what were they smoking when they did it?

I have rarely been as terrified as I was when I resolved to somehow power across that figure-eight from hell. I started by going round and round the first circle, working my way to the outside lane, getting honked at, of course, and sweating enough to soak my shirt. I had gone around that circle three or four times when the traffic thinned enough that I found the courage to dive into the second circle...and wound up going counterclockwise, the way we would just about anywhere outside Britain's sphere of influence.

Cars careened toward me, horns blared, bright white teeth formed ugly words. I aimed for the curb, jumped it, and stopped short in the grass while trying to catch my breath. Holy sh— My heart was staccato. I gave it some minutes, and when all the witnesses to my ineptitude had negotiated their way away, I dropped back onto the road, going clockwise this time, exited at the road to Basseterre and proceeded on, feeling as relieved as I would have if I'd survived a plane crash.

Soon I was in the older part of town, buildings of chaos and volcanic stone block. I went round and round a central square, an open-air mall, an old stone church, cubbies of businesses in narrow storefronts, the cruise ship port, its gleaming modern stores and eateries secured for passengers only behind tall chain-link fences.

I found my place to park, got out on foot and went exploring. There was supposed to be a bookstore in Basseterre, one of the main things I had been looking forward to, but that store proved to be long gone and, as I was told by a resident, there was no other.

I spent a couple of hours walking around Basseterre. After the quiet of Nevis, Basseterre overwhelmed me. Getting hungry, I went into a few local restaurants but they were all jammed full, no way to decompress, study the menus and figure the places out. I eventually migrated back to the scooter, took a route out of town that bypassed those crazy traffic circles, had a great lunch at Poinciana Restaurant in Kittian Village, then proceeded back to the Sea Bridge ferry port. I arrived much too early, so I took a side road around to the Reggae Beach Bar and Grill, where a few beers settled my still-shaken nerves. I bought a "Rush Slowly" T-shirt, laughed and felt much better.

I'm glad I came, but doubt I will again until I leave.

WEDNESDAY, FEBRUARY 15, 2017

Southern Comfort

I must have caught something in Basseterre. I'm sneezing, coughing, and feel like hell. Still managed to do some work on Chapter Eleven.

It was so clear today that I could see the part of Montserrat that was blown away in that volcanic eruption in the 90s. Wow.

FRIDAY, FEBRUARY 17, 2017

Southern Comfort

Another flu. I soaked the sheets yesterday, but feel somewhat better today. Finished Chapter Eleven. Some spicy curry from Indian Summer should clear my sinuses and help me recover.

THURSDAY, FEBRUARY 23, 2017

Southern Comfort

Chapter Twelve is finished. Took the scooter down to the Botanical Gardens and toured the grounds. Very nice, quiet and calming. Had lunch at the Oasis, a Thai restaurant there. The food was very good.

MONDAY, FEBRUARY 27, 2017

Four Seasons Resort

I'm kind of stalled on Chapter Thirteen, so I walked away from it and came here to the Four Season Resort for a spa day. I've never done this before, but I have enjoyed myself, and I feel great! I was in the sauna for a while, and then a massage, and now I'm eating a great lunch next to a pretty pond while dressed in a cotton bathrobe. Curious that no one else is here—off-season, I guess—but I do enjoy the solitude.

SUNDAY, MARCH 5, 2017

Southern Comfort

This has been a gorgeous day. Montserrat and Redonda are sharp and clear on the horizon. Could have gone for a ride, but decided to stay in to finish Chapter Thirteen. I've got to start cutting back on groceries now. Time grows short. It's a little depressing. Hard to keep my mind on the novel and off having to leave soon.

View of Montserrat and Redonda from Southern Comfort

TUESDAY, MARCH 7, 2017

Alexander Hamilton Museum, Charlestown

Ferocious wind and heavy rain overnight. Did some work on Chapter Fourteen, then went to Cafe des Arts for lunch. Now I am at the Alexander Hamilton Museum. How many people know that one of our Founding Fathers was born right here in Charlestown? I did, but only because I've read Hamilton's biography. The curators are very proud of this heritage, and have done the best they can with what they have to work with. I donated some money, and was really disappointed that our government hasn't done anything to help support them.

SATURDAY, MARCH 18, 2017

Southern Comfort

Hard rain overnight and this morning. The TV and internet are out. Wrote a few lines of dialog, but still haven't found a way to make

Chapter Fourteen work. It's so hard to focus now. Went to Indian Summer for lunch, and then to the Double Deuce to see Shelisa and make a reservation for my final Yorkshire-Pudding Sunday on Nevis.

MONDAY, MARCH 20, 2017

Cycle World, Oualie

Left Chapter Fourteen to languish.

Got up early and cycled around to Oualie to help Winston with a group ride. His usual assistant couldn't make it, so I volunteered to help. Apparently these tours are how Winston makes a good percentage of his income.

There were ten or eleven people, all off a cruise ship, I think, and only on the island for the rest of the day. We started out by fitting them on their bikes, which are mountain bikes, the very bikes Winston and I built a while back. Winston then took the lead, with me following behind to look after any stragglers.

The ride was mostly on dirt, on mountain bike trails that I've seen on the map but never ventured onto myself since I prefer road cycling. Nevertheless, my CAADX is built for off-road use, with sturdy wheels and mountain-bike gearing, so I had no problem. There wasn't much climb in this ride, that is not what these folks are here for, but rather to see some sights off the main road and get a little exercise at the same time.

All of the ride took place between Oualie and Lovers Beach, which is that black sand beach this side of the airport. It's a shame in a way. Remembering that this is the dry side of the island, if these folks have spent all of their time at Oualie Beach then they haven't experienced the tropical nature of Nevis at all. A few even asked me about that, curious when they learned that I was staying on the opposite side of the island. How often does it rain? they asked. Almost every night, I answered, hence "rainforest." Do I ever see the monkeys? All the time, I answered. Although there is a "Monkey Crossing" sign near here, none of the folks I spoke with had seen a monkey.

We toured some old church ruins, then proceeded overland to a promontory with an amazing view toward St. Kitts. People took their photos and selfies and then it was time to head back, which we did on the road rather than overland. I wondered about this. There's a pretty good little hill in this stretch of road, nothing like the Killer Bee or the climb to Gingerland, but enough that many of these people wouldn't be able to make it. Winston went on with the stronger cyclists, while I held back. At the base of the hill, several of my riders got off to push, so I got off as well, pushed with them and made conversation.

I enjoyed this day. It was like spending a day at one of the national parks I've worked at, doing interpretation for the visitors. I've learned enough about Nevis that I was able to answer their questions competently, and hopefully educate them a bit as well. I wish I could do this again, but there won't be time.

TUESDAY, MARCH 21, 2017

Cafe des Arts

Time isn't trickling away now, it's rushing down the Killer Bee.

I spent a good part of the day mailing a box of books home. I've read quite a few since I've been here, and while I could gallantly leave these books in the villa for the next guest, I'm a bibliophile, and so—you know—gotta keep everything I read, a gentle madness as they say.

I did finally succeed after much red tape and misdirection. The cost? About $44.00 USD, and by gosh you'd better tape the corners just right!

Had lunch at the Double Deuce, then back to the villa to kind of clean and put things away and pretend that I'm at peace with my departure next week.

Now I'm at Cafe des Arts for Burger Night, not my last because I'll still be here next Tuesday, but the last for Ross, a man I've met. He's headed back to Scotland tomorrow, Dumfries, I think. I'm going to miss his accent. Even though I've still got some time, I feel as if Ross and I are facing the gallows together. Time to tie one on in proper Scots fashion.

WEDNESDAY, MARCH 22, 2017

Southern Comfort

Haven't been this hungover in a long time. Think I'll stay in bed today.

THURSDAY, MARCH 23, 2017

Southern Comfort

Some light editing on Chapter Fourteen, but it needs more work. Went for a counterclockwise ride. It felt great to sweat out some of the overindulgence left over from Tuesday.

FRIDAY MARCH 24, 2017

Indian Summer

Finished Chapter Fourteen finally! I guess this will be the last chapter I write on Nevis. I'm now on my goodbye tour, having my last lunch at Indian Summer, chicken curry, of course, extra spicy and with another Guinness, just to aid digestion, don't you know.

SATURDAY, MARCH 25, 2017

Southern Comfort

Went for my final bike ride on Nevis, counterclockwise as usual. While I did master the Gingerland climb, I'm disappointed that I was never able to stay on the bike all the way up the Killer Bee. If I ever return to Nevis, I'll bring my Cannondale Synapse. It has triple cranks, extra gearing that may help me conquer that killer climb.

For now, I need to get the CAADX cleaned and ready. Winston is going to buy it from me. It costs so much to get high-end bikes to the island, and it's so much hassle breaking them down and shipping them out, that I thought this was a good way to go. I rode this bike in Korea and Scandinavia, so I'm going to miss it, but it will do great service here.

SUNDAY, MARCH 26, 2017

Double Deuce

The goodbye tour continues. Did cleaning and laundry and some packing, and now I'm at the Double Deuce, saying goodbye to Shelisa and Julie and enjoying my last Yorkshire Pudding on Nevis.

Shelisa has been a good sport about the character I based on her, although I can tell she's a little wary. I promised to send her a copy of the novel as soon as it's published.

MONDAY, MARCH 27, 2017

Southern Comfort

Stayed in and packed even though the day is gorgeous. Winston came by to pick up the CAADX. We probably won't see one another again. We shook hands and promised to keep in touch.

TUESDAY, MARCH 28, 2017

Cafe des Arts

All this time on the island, and I never went swimming until today. What an idiot I am.

I took the scooter around to Herbert's Beach, which is east around the turn from Nisbet Beach and the airport. This beach is far from the road, through sand and palm trees and brush. The water is aqua, shallow and soft, and there was no one else around. No one! So I dropped trou and everything else and dove in, swam for an hour then dried in the sun. I heard a rumor that skinny dipping is illegal on Nevis, but I got away with it without incident.

The goodbye tour continues. I had my last lunch at Yubrenta's Snackette, and now my last Burger Night at Cafe des Arts. I'm going to miss the expat crowd here.

WEDNESDAY, MARCH 29, 2017

Southern Comfort

Took a last ride around the island on the scooter, just trying to imprint all of it. I have to give the scooter back to Kevin tomorrow.

Had a last lunch and look-around at the Oasis Botanical Gardens.

THURSDAY, MARCH 30, 2017

Last Day

Started getting things ready. Turned in the keys and gave the scooter (sadly) back to Kevin. Winston showed up, so I got to have a final, final lunch with him at Yubrenta's Snackette. I went for the salt fish, to remind me of my first lunch there.

This is it, then. I guess I'm ready to go.

FRIDAY, MARCH 31, 2017

Houston, Texas

Up at 3:30 a.m., out the door by 4:15 a.m. Raul picked me up in his taxi and drove me around to Oualie for the water taxi, which carried me across The Narrows in the dark, to Daisy and her taxi awaiting on the other side. Daisy got me to the airport in plenty of time, zipping through that double traffic circle as if it were the most natural thing in the world.

Our plane broke so we were delayed 1½ hours, but still made it to Miami on time. Caught my Houston flight and arrived in the dark, although a different dark than this morning. I have no idea what time it is. The traffic is garish, frightening. The noise, the smell. Man, this place is hell.

Where's the rum?

2018

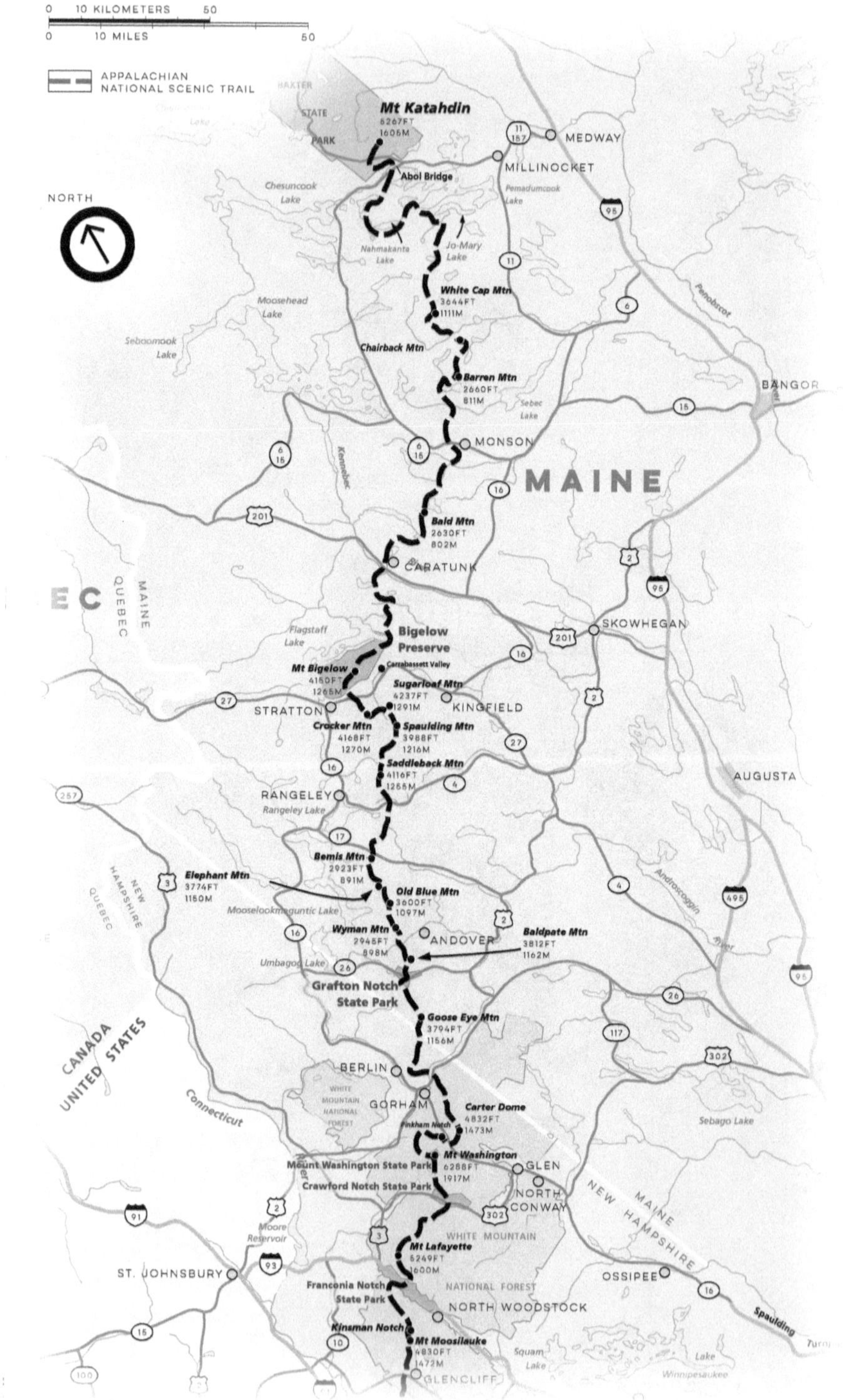
0 10 KILOMETERS 50
0 10 MILES 50
APPALACHIAN NATIONAL SCENIC TRAIL
NORTH
BAXTER STATE PARK
Mt Katahdin
5267FT
1605M
Abol Bridge
MEDWAY
MILLINOCKET
Chesuncook Lake
Pemadumcook Lake
Nahmakanta Lake
Jo-Mary Lake
White Cap Mtn
3644FT
1111M
Moosehead Lake
Seboomook Lake
Chairback Mtn
Barren Mtn
2660FT
811M
Sebec Lake
Penobscot
BANGOR
MONSON
Kennebec
MAINE
Bald Mtn
2630FT
802M
CARATUNK
MAINE
QUEBEC
EC
SKOWHEGAN
Flagstaff Lake
Bigelow Preserve
Carrabassett Valley
Mt Bigelow
4150FT
1265M
Sugarloaf Mtn
4237FT
1291M
STRATTON
KINGFIELD
Crocker Mtn
4168FT
1270M
Spaulding Mtn
3988FT
1216M
Saddleback Mtn
4116FT
1255M
RANGELEY
Rangeley Lake
AUGUSTA
Bemis Mtn
2923FT
891M
Elephant Mtn
3774FT
1150M
NEW HAMPSHIRE
QUEBEC
Old Blue Mtn
3600FT
1097M
Mooselookmeguntic Lake
Androscoggin River
Wyman Mtn
2945FT
898M
ANDOVER
Baldpate Mtn
3812FT
1162M
Umbagog Lake
Grafton Notch State Park
Goose Eye Mtn
3794FT
1156M
CANADA
UNITED STATES
BERLIN
WHITE MOUNTAIN NATIONAL FOREST
GORHAM
Connecticut
Carter Dome
4832FT
1473M
Pinkham Notch
Sebago Lake
Mt Washington
6288FT
1917M
Mount Washington State Park
GLEN
Crawford Notch State Park
NORTH CONWAY
NEW HAMPSHIRE
MAINE
River
Moore Reservoir
WHITE MOUNTAIN
Mt Lafayette
5249FT
1600M
ST. JOHNSBURY
OSSIPEE
NATIONAL FOREST
Franconia Notch State Park
NORTH WOODSTOCK
Spaulding Turnpike
Kinsman Notch
Mt Moosilauke
4830FT
1472M
Squam Lake
Lake Winnipesaukee
GLENCLIFF

I spent the remainder of 2017 at home, looking after the farm, then took up my novel again over the winter, finishing it in the spring of 2018. The Latter Half of Inglorious Years *was published just days before I departed for something that had been approaching on my calendar for a decade, the fulfillment of a promise I had made to myself—a third thru-hike of the Appalachian Trail.*

SUNDAY, APRIL 22, 2018

Smith County, Tennessee

When I promised myself in 2008 that I would return for another Appalachian Trail thru-hike in 2018...well, I never realized how quickly a decade could pass. And anyway, 2018 sounded back then like science fiction, not reality. Surely that date would never come, but then if it did appear one New Year's morning, maybe a bus would have taken me out by then, or a heart attack, or a round from an assault rifle. Family and friends well acquainted with the evening news (or perhaps a stifling succession of news feeds) fret about my welfare on a hike like this. I don't. And besides, if something were to happen to me I would rather face it on the Appalachian Trail than elsewhere in the banal times we now inhabit.

To recap:

I hiked the Appalachian Trail in 2001, was given the trail name "Solo" by the rangers at Baxter State Park in the state of Maine, then proceeded over the next four months and some to discover every frailty inherent in my body and spirit. That hike was a soul-searching mess. When it was over, I was dispirited, fifty pounds lighter, and couldn't walk without a wobble. Within days though, with some food and a little rest, I began to berate myself for leaving the trail early. My mind was in a new place, no longer right between my shoulders but just a little to the left, where I was not always able to keep an eye on my mouth. This inability to self-censor caused me some personal and professional headaches, but I found that I didn't care. Real life was on a trail in the mountains; everything else was just distraction.

My failure to complete the Appalachian Trail in one thru-hike ate at me in every waking moment. There was not a day that I didn't recall some portion of that experience; not a day that I didn't want to go back. I thru-hiked again in 2008, turned 50 on the trail, and was so startled by my physical and mental transformation that I didn't want that hike to end even as I raced toward that end with thirty-mile-plus days, light on my feet and feeling years younger. It was amazing.

I rocked the trail in 2008, finished on the very day I left it in 2001, September 27. It would be serendipitous if that happened again, but it wasn't a goal in 2008 or a goal now. It would be cool, though, no doubt about it.

Hiking southbound once again, I expect to turn 60 somewhere in lower Maine. Ten years on, but I feel pretty well. I'm anxious only because of my age, but if this hike is anything like my 2008 hike, all of that anxiety will be dispelled by the time I clear the Hundred-Mile Wilderness. Of real concern is the wave after wave of bad weather New England experienced this past winter. It might be difficult to climb Mt. Katahdin because of snow, and White Cap Mountain might be impassable. So, starting with a base weight of twelve pounds, I'm going to add some extra cold-weather gear and hope that I'm better prepared for cold conditions than I was in 2008.

Time draws near.

"Solo," headin' south.

Always forward, never backward, and pass every white blaze.

ME→GA '01   ME→GA '08   ME→GA '18

TUESDAY, MAY 15, 2018

Medway, Maine

It has been a day. Up at 3:00 a.m., out the door at 4:00 a.m. Bryan's mother, who volunteered to take me on the ninety-minute drive to the Nashville airport, was already out front waiting, looking perky for such an early hour. I was still in a fog, myself. Before we pulled away, she seemed to become subdued, looking away, looking at her hands, looking at nothing through the dark windshield. She eventually handed me a small container in a ziplock bag. "Would you—?" she asked hesitantly. "If it's not—if it's not too much trouble?"

"Of course I will," I said.

I never met Bryan Winfree, but through correspondences over a few months, I did feel that I was coming to know him. Bryan was giving serious thought to thru-hiking the Appalachian Trail. He contacted me for advice in the spring of 2013, and for a short time, through his youth and enthusiasm, I was able to relive vicariously my own Appalachian Trail adventures. We discussed gear and conditions and philosophies, and even some deeper thoughts, as when he wrote me:

> *My initial trepidations are pretty cliche I suppose at this point: quitting a perfectly good job, leaving my family, girlfriend, and dogs behind, all for a selfish desire to go find myself, while also accomplishing something I can only imagine would be one of the greatest things I ever achieve in my life. I tend to be a dreamer about certain things and I get big ideas that seem idyllic, but I have to believe that I would come out a much better version of myself than I currently find myself to be.*

2014 was to be his year. I swelled with pride when he informed me that he intended to hike southbound, to seek the solitude of the sobo thru-hiker, along with the heightened physical challenge. I looked forward to meeting him in person, perhaps see him off on his journey, perhaps join him at the end at Springer Mountain, Georgia to witness how the journey had honed him, matured him, made him larger.

Bryan was killed in a freak automobile accident on December 21, 2013. He was twenty-seven years old. I had come down with a terrible cold, but pushed through the fever and chills to attend the celebration of Bryan's life. Afraid that I might spread my cold, I didn't stay long. I left behind a small Appalachian Trail medallion, the connection we shared, the only way I knew to honor him.

More than four years later, that medallion is sewn into the fabric of my backpack, where it will travel from one end of the Appalachian Trail to the other in memory of Bryan and his dream. And now, his mother's hesitant request, followed by my immediate answer: Of course I will carry Bryan's ashes with me on the Appalachian Trail, I'm honored to do it, and when I finish and bring his ashes home, he will have made his hike as well.

The rest is pretty much routine by now, the journey to the northern terminus of the Appalachian Trail following the same stages as my previous hikes: the flight to Boston Logan; the Concord Bus within the hour to Portland, Maine; the two hour wait for the bus to Bangor; the Cyr Bus within the hour to Medway, Maine, arriving as the sun was setting; the stay at the Medway Gateway Inn—and it's still the same day! Amazing.

I'm starting a week earlier this time hoping to get ahead of the blackflies. I'll shuttle into the park tomorrow morning.

WEDNESDAY, MAY 16, 2018

Rainbow Stream Shelter - 15 Miles

Checked out of the hotel at 6:00 a.m. feeling very well. The weather is great, clear and crisp, but rumor has it that Mt. Katahdin is still closed. Not to worry, I'll stealth up if I have to. Nothing new there.

A guy named Chris shuttled me in. It turns out that not only is Mt. Katahdin closed, but the road into Baxter State Park as well. I could still stealth K, after a long hike from the park boundary to the Hunt trailhead, but Chris has convinced me not to do it. Apparently there has been some bad behavior on K these past few years, enough that the park managers have threatened to close Mt. Katahdin to thru-hikers. If they caught me stealthing up the mountain, Chris fears, it might be the final event that tips the park managers over the edge.

I am shocked. I had no idea that any of this had been going on. Chris reinforced his concerns. "This park belongs to the state of Maine, not the National Park Service," he said, giving me a stern look. "If they want Katahdin off the Appalachian Trail, then it's off the Appalachian Trail."

This was not idle speculation, Chris was serious, his tone a shade short of chiding me. I sighed. My options were few: I could either

Rainbow Ledges Overlooking Mt. Katahdin

sit in Millinocket for a week or more waiting for the park to open, or I could begin my hike at Abol Bridge just outside the park, then shuttle back from Monson after I cleared the Hundred-Mile Wilderness. Neither option was appealing. There was no way I could sit idle for even a few days let alone weeks, so that option was out, while starting at Abol Bridge seemed an inauspicious way to begin such a long journey. But what choice did I have? The more I thought about the situation in Baxter State Park, and with my previous hikes making me feel more like an elder statesman on this journey, there was no way I would risk allowing myself to become the final straw that closed the park.

"Take me to Abol Bridge," I reluctantly conceded. "I'll shuttle back from Monson to do K."

Chris exhaled in relief, and complied, and deposited me at Abol Bridge at 9:45 a.m.

The weather was even more glorious when I started out, cool and startlingly clear. Leaving almost a week earlier than I usually start my hikes, though, the woods look different, still bare such that I felt as if I were shuffling through a jumble of autumn leaves. I made good time, Hurd Brook by 11:00 a.m., and then the Rainbow Ledges by lunchtime, where I got a look back at a snow-free Mt. Katahdin. "Why is the park still closed?" I grumbled. "It looks great up there."

I made it to Rainbow Stream shelter by 5:30 p.m., all alone with the gurgling stream and the soothing forest sounds. I had to laugh. Although Rainbow Stream shelter figures prominently in my novel, *The Appalachian*, I had never actually stayed in this shelter. Starting at Abol Bridge rather than Katahdin Stream Campground gave me a head start of about ten miles, so I have made it that much farther. I'll have to make those miles up when I shuttle back, but they're easy, fast miles.

Anyway, maybe leaving from Abol Bridge wasn't so inauspicious after all. I mean, Rainbow Stream shelter is *really* important in my novel. I ought to at least be able to say that I had stayed there; but if I had climbed K today, I would have either stayed at Katahdin Stream Campground or Daicey Pond. I would have made Hurd Brook shelter the next day, and then on from there, passing Rainbow Stream shelter on my way to the shelter at Wadleigh Stream.

So things work out. I hiked strong today—no blisters, no bug bites—and now I can lighten my pack by about two pounds. I carried a copy of *The Appalachian* with me to leave here at the shelter. At 750 pages, it felt as if I were carrying a two-pound brick along with everything else. It's so heavy that no hiker would want to pack it out of here. I just hope hikers read it and enjoy it, and don't use it in the privy or to start their campfires.

THURSDAY, MAY 17, 2018

Potaywadjo Spring Shelter – 18.2 Miles

Up at first light, 4:30 a.m., cold but bearable. This is my first stay at Potaywadjo shelter. Starting at Abol Bridge is completely reordering my transit of the Hundred-Mile Wilderness, but that's okay. Now I can get some new experiences.

I was on the trail by 6:00 a.m., then made a long 8 miles to Wadleigh Stream shelter for lunch at 11:30. Five hours but only 8 miles...it was a slow slog on a boggy trail and with some blowdowns. I forgot that Nesuntabunt Mountain was in this section, where I sprained my ankle so badly on my 2008 hike. The climbs weren't hard, but enough to slow my pace. I was extra careful in the slippery section where I sprained my ankle. I remembered it precisely.

I thought I was making a better pace afterward, but I didn't get here until 6:00 p.m. Those were 18.2 hard-fought miles, the usual roots and rocks and climbs that never seem as bad when you think back on them.

I'm alone, haven't seen anyone except a MATC (Maine Appalachian Trail Club) volunteer on Rainbow Ledges. Was that yesterday? Time is so elastic on the trail.

Anyway, I feel fine. A little weary. This is a warm spot, so it's a little buggy in the shelter.

FRIDAY, MAY 18, 2018

Cooper Brook Falls Shelter - 11.4 Miles

Forty degrees this morning, which made my coffee that much more enjoyable. I'm going to have to start rationing fuel, though, because I have not brought enough to get me through the Wilderness. I don't know how I screwed this up. I don't want to hike out for resupply like I had to do in 2008, but I don't think rationing will get me to Monson.

I made Jo Mary Road by noon, 7.6 miles in four hours. Not a great pace, but conditions haven't been great either. I saw some MATC volunteers by the road, so I went over to see if I could yogi some fuel. I scored sixteen ounces of Coleman fuel from them, which should be enough, so now I don't have to hike out.

Afterward, we all sat around and talked. They were waiting on extra gear to be brought in, so had time to kill. I told them about my previous hikes, which impressed them. They named me a trail ambassador, and asked if I would help educate the nobos I encountered about the "Finish Well" etiquette on Mt. Katahdin. I had seen a post-er about this in one of the shelters. This is how the trail managers hope to overcome the problems they've been having.

"Sure," I said. "Proud to."

Then I told them Bryan's story, that I carried Bryan's ashes, and that he was making the hike with me in spirit. This sobered the group.

"He needs a trail name," one of them said.

"Yeah," said another.

It had never occurred to me, but what a great idea. They pondered for a while, and then one of them offered: "I know—Freewind! Call him Freewind."

What a perfect, perfect trail name for Bryan! From now on, I'm going to sign *Freewind* in every trail register.

I left them finally and slipped back into the woods. A tendon in my left foot started to ache, so I pulled in here early to soak my feet in the cold stream. My left foot is swollen. I have no idea why.

SATURDAY, MAY 19, 2018

Logan Brook Shelter – 11.7 Miles

Thirty-eight degrees this morning. My fingers are so stiff I can barely write, but at least the swelling has gone down in my foot. I have no idea what that was about.

Started out strong, fooling myself that I could pull a 19 and clear White Cap Mountain today. It could have been possible, but I encountered a couple of miles of blowdowns, the worst I've ever seen. I couldn't get through all the tangled limbs with my backpack on, so I had to toss it ahead, along with my trekking poles, then climb and duck and weave my way through the cloying limbs, retrieve my backpack then toss it again. This went on for hours, so by the time I reached Logan Brook shelter, after only 11.7 miles, I was completely worn out, as well as scratched and scuffed and generally miserable.

As an irony, I ran into some MATC volunteers at the end of this mess, who were working fast with chainsaws to clear the trail. I told them how bad it was behind me, which they acknowledged with sighs. It's behind me now, but still ahead for them. As fast as they're working, though, I bet they have it all cleared by tomorrow. So this is the downside of leaving early for a southbound hike.

On the plus side, I found a pair of flip-flops to wear in camp, the very superlight kind that I couldn't find in stores before I left. I saw one on the ground all by itself, took it, and in the midst of the blowdowns some miles later, found the other one. Ha! They fit perfectly, and give example to my rule: never strap things to the outside of your pack.

SUNDAY, MAY 20, 2018

Carl A. Newhall Shelter – 7.2 Miles

This is the day I started my 2008 hike. No congratulations, though, White Cap Mountain kicked my butt anyway!

I was on the trail at 6:00 a.m., feeling well and moving fast. It wasn't long, though, before I hit snow so deep that I had to post-hole through. This was much worse than I have seen it before, and what I had been afraid of after all of those winter storms. I just gritted my teeth and waded through, making a half mile an hour at best, thinking conditions couldn't get worse. Then it began to rain.

The summit was socked in, couldn't see anything. I have a great photo on this summit from my 2008 hike. It was sunny and warm that time. I met a couple of weekend hikers, a father-son team, and was able to yogi some food from them. In these tough conditions, I'm burning calories faster than I expected, so now I'm short on food. I'll run out if I don't pick up the pace.

Nevertheless, after only 7.2 miles I was spent. I threw down at Newhall shelter, completely exhausted. A couple of guys came in about an hour later, Dylan and Andrew. They just graduated from college and are hiking the Hundred-Mile Wilderness northbound as a final adventure together before they go off on their careers. These are the first people I've shared a shelter with on this hike. They're good guys.

I like them. They gave me some of their ramen, which was nice, and we talked late into the evening. Andrew is a graphic designer, and Dylan will be going overseas with the Peace Corps for a few years.

A funny story about these guys: Andrew lost his spork on their first day out, so once their camp meal was cooked, each would take a turn with their single spoon. Andrew would take a bite then offer the spoon to Dylan, who would take a bite and then hand the spoon back to Andrew. This was hilarious to watch. I laughed, they explained everything to me, and then, as Andrew was telling their tale, his eyes focused in on the trail-register box, and lying there, right on top, was a spoon!

It was a great coincidence, and it lightened our evening. I have a feeling that Andrew will always hang on to that spoon.

MONDAY, MAY 21, 2018

Cloud Pond Shelter – 16.8 Miles

This is the day I started my hike in 2001. I only made it as far as Daicey Pond that day. Fifty-pound backpack. I remember that Kelty Super Tioga external frame well, sold it to a Navajo guy at a yard sale in Page, Arizona in 2005.

I hiked out at 7:00 a.m., lingering a bit longer than normal over breakfast while talking with Dylan and Andrew.

In contrast to the snow, it got damn hot today, hot enough that the blackflies came out in swarms, worse than I have ever experienced them. Despite the heat, I put on my thick Capilene shirt and then eventually my rain shell as well, cinching the hood around my face. The blackflies descended in literal clouds, so thick that I wiped them from my face like blowing sand. It was hard to breathe without inhaling them, and I did inhale quite a few. They are acrid at the back of the throat. One caught in my windpipe, making me cough hard enough to retch before I could get it out.

I wound a bandana around my face, but with so many layers on in the heat, the bandana quickly became soaked with sweat. I couldn't breathe so I had to take it off, taking gulps of breath through my palm while wiping the blackflies out of my face every few steps.

OH—MY—GOD, what a biblical plague!

I have bites all around my neck and wrists where my clothes cinched down. Nothing worked this time, not cigar smoke, not DEET—nothing. I was actually glad when I got to Chairback Mountain, scrambling up those rocks like a goat, praying it would be cool enough up top to drive off the bugs.

It wasn't cool enough on top, and on top of that, one of my shoes came apart during the climb. The sole peeled right off while I was crabbing up a steep granite incline. I have never had anything like this happen before. What crap quality!

As a double blow (or triple? quadruple? I lost count), this area is in a rain shadow, very dry. I searched twenty minutes for the spring at Chairback Gap shelter, gave up in a swarm of blackflies and never found it.

I didn't reach Cloud Pond shelter until 7:30 p.m., grungy, bitten, dehydrated—F—! A hammock was strung right behind the shelter. I hollered my approach, but no one responded. Cloud Pond had been my favorite shelter on the Appalachian Trail, but things have changed in ten years. That gorgeous view of the pond, where I have watched moose dip their shaggy heads, is now completely obscured by the understory; and the shelter itself has sagged so that the floor is canted toward the back.

What a disappointment, but I was too tired to whine about it. I pulled off my duct-taped shoes, swallowed cold ramen, and then breaking my own rule, got into my sleeping bag without washing up first. So now my bag will be funky, but I was too damn tired to care.

Before nodding off, a girl came around from the hammock to introduce herself. Her name was Sharon or Shannon, I can't remember which. She was young twenties, cute, was from Bangor but had never been in this part of her state. She said I was the first thru-hiker she had ever met, and would I mind answering some questions about the thru-hiking mentality? I said no, I didn't mind. We thru-hikers love to talk about ourselves, after all, especially with pretty, young women in the Hundred-Mile Wilderness. I guess something in my look revealed my more lascivious thoughts because she quickly appended that her boyfriend was asleep in their hammock just beyond the wall I was propped against.

We wound up talking for quite a while. Her questions ranged widely, giving me the impression that she was a grad student, sociology or maybe anthropology. She headed back to her hammock when it became too dark to see, feeling her way along the shelter wall. I heard their zipper pull, the rocking squeak as she hauled herself into the hammock. I heard voices, nothing coherent, just soft talk between her and her boyfriend. And then some shuffling, and then squeak-squeak, squeak-squeak, squeak-squeak, occasionally a low moan, like a sigh of wind on a mountaintop. I cleared my throat, and the squeaking came to a stop as abruptly as a hammer against a nail.

And then I chuckled myself to sleep.

TUESDAY, MAY 22, 2018

Monson, Maine – 19.1 Miles

I did not sleep well at all, kept sliding to the back of the shelter and fetching against the wall, like gravity folding me into a corner. Up at 4:30 a.m., used the last of my food to make a half-ramen, half-energy bar breakfast. Out of coffee, that was the worst. Waved a silent goodbye at 6:00 a.m. to the amorous hammockers, still sleeping in the gentle lullaby of love.

It's a good thing I started early, else I would have been forsaken and screwed and worse. The forest was Faustian, full of bogs and bugs and climbs and slips and falls and suffocating blackflies. There were four river fords, I think, and rock scramble after rock scramble after rock scramble. The blackflies were a tempest that darkened the sky, so thick and suffocating that at one point I dropped pack and lay in the trail, curled in my rain shell for even a moment's reprieve, driven onward finally only because it was so hot, and I was so hungry, and the water in the area was so bad.

A beaver dam had flooded the trail, I mean a big lake of brown, nasty, beaver shit-infested water that I tried to circumnavigate but was eventually forced to wade through, only ankle-deep but sometimes I would sink into mud up to my calves. Nasty! And then, pulling a foot from the mud for my next step, my foot came out of my shoe, which was down in there somewhere and I had to balance and bend over and fish for it. Oh, man, really nasty!

Conditions were so bad that I took out my phone when I got to a dry spot, powered it up and was fully prepared to beg for a shuttle out of the Wilderness at the next logging road, maybe a mile or so away. I look back now and am quite relieved that I couldn't get a cell signal, because I don't know how I would have been able to live with myself if I'd had to be rescued. Even more embarrassing, when I couldn't get a signal I tried 911. OH—THANK—GOD I couldn't get a signal!

I reached Leeman Brook shelter at 5:30 p.m. after twelve and a half hours of some of the most miserable hiking I have ever endured. The road to Monson was only three miles away, but I believed I would not survive if I took one more step. I fell into the shelter, bringing my cloud of blackflies with me, curled up in my rain shell and listened as they dive-bombed me—tick, tick, tick, tick, tick...like a rain of little pellets. Man, it was hot. Hadn't I just been post-holing through snow? When was that? Yesterday? A week ago? I couldn't remember, but I did remember being cold at some point, my fingers too stiff to write.

I lay there in the stifling heat, the blackfly offensive ongoing. My stomach growled, and then again, a painful spasm. I had no food, no calories whatsoever, enough fuel left to boil a few ounces of this tainted water, but nothing more. I hauled myself up, waved the blackflies out of my face, and muttered, "The hell with this."

I had lain there for thirty minutes. It was now 6:00 p.m., late in the day but still bright this time of year. With pure, stubborn determination, I shouldered my pack, took up my trekking poles, and got away from that shelter as fast as the trail would let me.

More climbs—even the least incline seemed to draw the last measure from me. It took me two agonizing hours to make those last three miles. It was still light when I crunched onto the gravel parking area at Maine Route 15. The blackflies stayed in the woods, as if too afraid to come out into the clear. I sat down at the edge of the road, propped against a rock. It began to rain, cool and clean, and I turned my face into it and licked it off my lips. It felt so good to be able to breathe, to be free of the blackflies. It might be too late to get a hitch into Monson, but I would have been satisfied to fall asleep right there in the wet, clean air.

A guy pulled up, gentle rain misting in the glare of his headlights. He reached across, opened the passenger door and hollered, "Do you need a ride into Monson?" I smiled and nodded and got in, feeling bad that I was getting his seats wet, but he didn't seem to mind.

It was well after dark when we got into Monson, but the rain had ceased. The town was quiet. I had him drop me at Shaw's Hostel, where I have always stayed. I knew Keith Shaw, he helped me out in 2001. I can still remember his gravelly laugh. I learned in 2008 that he had passed away, although some local ladies were keeping the hostel going. I wondered what I would find in 2018—

—I found that Shaw's was now owned by Poet and Hippy Chick, a pair of northbounders whom I had met in 2008, I think at the Mayor's house in New York. They, however, were down in Virginia for Trail Days, and so Shaw's was currently closed. Feeling despondent but not desperate—I had consulted my AWOL trail guide, so knew there was another hostel in Monson—I went to Lakeshore House Lodge and Pub nearby, which was closed for the day although light still shone through the windows. I pounded on the door, now feeling desperate. Fortunately someone heard me, and within minutes I was being hugged by Rebekah, the enthusiastic owner, who said I was her first thru-hiker of the season. Minutes after that I was drinking a cold beer while showering (deeply satisfying, by the way), and minutes after that I was eating the biggest, best plank of roast beef that has ever been laid before me.

Now in my bunk, feeling comfortable, full, and clean, I try to return my mind to this morning at Cloud Pond, some sixteen hours or so ago, hours that seem like days, now too distant to matter.

That's the way it is on the trail. What's behind is behind, there is only forward.

WEDNESDAY, MAY 23, 2018

Lakeshore House, Monson, Maine – Zero

I slept until 7:00 a.m., a luxurious indulgence for me. I'm the only one here, so it's quiet. I feel pretty well, albeit a little sore in places.

There is a lot I need to do. I'll go out for resupply anon, but first I need coffee and food, and then more coffee and more food. I need to do laundry, and I should spin my sleeping bag in the dryer to get the funk out, along with any hitchhikers that might have crawled in. I need to see what I can do about these shoes.

Later—

I contacted the shoe company. They will not stand by their product, calling it "normal wear and tear." What a load of—well, you know. I'm going to shuttle into Greenville tomorrow to buy a new pair. Also a head net and some gloves. These blackflies *will* be conquered. For now, time to head downstairs to the bar.

THURSDAY, MAY 24, 2018

Lakeshore House, Monson, Maine – Zero

Another zero day, but there's no hurry: the mountain is still closed. I shuttled into Greenville, bought the shoes and the other things. The shoes are Salomon Speed Cross 4. They are comfortable, and look much more durable than what I had. Hopefully I'll get some good miles out of them.

Poet and Hippy Chick are back. I went over to talk to them. We recognized each other's trail names, and pondered where we met. I still think it was at the Mayor's house in New York, but I guess it could have been anywhere a week north or south of there. I bought some resupply from Poet. He's opened an outdoor shop to go along with the hostel. I like what he's done with the place, but I'm going to stay at Lakeshore House just the same. I'm already there, they're treating me great, and I don't want to risk any hurt feelings.

FRIDAY, MAY 25, 2018

Millinocket, Maine – Zero

They're going to open the Hunt Trail tomorrow, so I have shuttled back to Millinocket. It was a two-hour drive (and somewhat costly), and so now most of the day is gone. There is nothing else to do but wait. Chris will shuttle me into the park in the morning.

SATURDAY, MAY 26, 2018

Mt. Katahdin to Abol Bridge – 15.1 + 5.2 Miles

It's something I have never actually seen during my other hikes because Mt. Katahdin had then been enshrouded in mist and fog and spatters of cold rain. All I could perceive then was a lot of hand-over-hand climbing, reaching for handholds, pulling up, squeezing between rocks, wedging feet into cracks, swinging a leg, finding another handhold, then pulling. White blazes appeared through the gloom at the last instant. I had no sense of anything, no perspective, no scale, only that next handhold, feet hidden below me in the mist. It took hours, perhaps more, any sense of distance irrelevant, time folded into another dimension where it didn't apply. Summiting had been anticlimactic: a weathered sign diffuse in wisps of fog, no photos, no view, a long, slippery journey down, all of this a purposeless expenditure of energy yet necessary in order to begin a proper hike.

But not this time.

The day was gray but not gauzy, the woods wet, the rocks slick. I caught an occasional view between trees toward other mountains and a spattering of lakes, views of some detail so I had hope that conditions would improve. I met a married couple from New Brunswick along the way, mid-thirties, perhaps a little more or a little less, he about to embark on his first thru-hike, she accompanying him for the climb up Katahdin, to be followed by a day in the Hundred-Mile Wilderness. Then, she said, she had to get back to work while her husband continued on, come what may.

They were nice people. I liked them. He was a bit heavy, though. No worries, he would lose that soon enough, but his backpack weighed 38 pounds. Of this he said he was proud, having pared to such a light weight. I winced but said nothing. The worst thing you can do on the Appalachian Trail (from a long list of worst things) is to offer unsolicited advice. We all find our own way by and by.

There was a rock he couldn't get over, too slick, too high. It was his short legs, he explained. I gave him a pull up—his wife wasn't strong enough—promised to see them on top, then took off up the trail. I never saw them again. Hikers told me that the couple had turned back, that the couple couldn't negotiate the rocks. Whether this meant that the man had given up his dream to thru-hike the trail or whether he was just skipping Katahdin for now I do not know. I want to think that they went down, through the campground and then into the Hundred-Mile Wilderness. There are other climbs, though, many of them almost as difficult as Katahdin, and many too remote to call for help. If he went on, I hope he is well.

All alone now, I finally cleared the tree line, could look up to see what I had never been able to see before. My gut twisted and I exclaimed, "*Holy crap! I climbed that?*"

Getting to the top of Katahdin is a borderline technical climb. Through the mist of my previous hikes, I hadn't realized that because I hadn't been able to see it coming. Good thing too, because the climb looks so intimidating from below that I might have skipped it, at least in 2001.

I pushed on, wary, caching my trekking poles to free my hands. I found alternate routes when I couldn't swing a leg up without pulling my groin, hopped with a tingling belly onto knife-edged rocks that would have seen me plummet if I had slipped. The Hunt Trail, from Katahdin Stream Campground to the top, is 5.2 miles. The first mile is easy and fast, the second is annoying but fast enough, the third finally breaks through the tree line, and the rest are mostly vertical or near so.

It took four and a half hours to get to the top, most spent in those final couple of miles, but at last, on my third visit, I could see! The cloud layer was high, revealing a procession of peaks down through the Hundred-Mile Wilderness, many of which I had climbed last week. I went to the Katahdin sign, waited in line to take photos. There were a lot of hikers on the summit so it was hard to get any alone time with the sign, but I was so thrilled just to be able to take in the view that I didn't mind. We were all sharing a great day, we had all made the same climb...well, some came up the Abol Trail but I'm told it's pretty tough, too.

I lingered, wanting to memorize every vista. There came a point when the crowd thinned to just me and a couple of intrepid young guys who were about to go down Knife's Edge even though the trailhead at the bottom was supposed to be closed. I could see that Knife's Edge was clear of snow, though, so their hike would probably be pretty awesome unless they got in trouble with a park ranger.

A sudden lull in the wind then silence. The two guys finished taking photos and were about to head out, and I had an idea I wasn't sure about but it felt right. I went up to them, told them about Freewind, and asked if they would take photos as I scattered some of his ashes.

"Absolutely," they said in unison. "We'd be proud."

I was still a bit uncertain. Bryan's mother and I hadn't talked about scattering his ashes, just that I would carry them the length of the trail and then return them, presumably intact, at the end of the hike. But it felt so right, the crowd filing away, the wind, which had been brisk, dropping off to nothing...I gave them my phone, stood on an outcropping of rock, then poured some of Freewind's ashes into my palm. I was nervous.

"I've never done this before," I told the guys.

"Don't worry," one of them said. "I'm doing photos and video so we won't miss it. Just throw them out. I've got you."

I did as he suggested, throwing them in an arc. I was surprised that I could hear Freewind's ashes sprinkling on the granite like soft rain. I backed away from the edge, turned to the guys.

"Good job," they said, handing me my phone.

"Thanks."

And with that, they turned and scrambled over the rocks, heading for Knife's Edge. I watched them go, watched as another crowd arrived at the summit and as the wind kicked back up. And then I turned myself, leaving a part of Freewind to carry on here.

Feeling energized, I hopped from rock to rock going down, knees twinging, recovered my trekking poles, then engaged that rooty, rocky trail. With gravity on my side, I made great time.

I was at Abol Bridge by 5:00 p.m., and in another of those weird trail juxtapositions, within the hour I was eating pizza and drinking Bangor Brown Ale and feeling that I must have made the climb days ago.

SUNDAY, MAY 27, 2018

Lakeshore House, Monson, Maine – Zero

I woke up this morning in Millinocket feeling a little sore but otherwise okay. The company that makes my blown-up shoes relented. They're shipping a replacement pair, which I will use farther down the trail.

I didn't get back to Monson until after noon, so decided to zero one more day and then hike out early tomorrow. My inability to climb K at the beginning, though, has cost me four zero days (well, three zero days because I would have needed at least one to recover from the Hundred-Mile Wilderness) as well as quite a bit of money. I've enjoyed my stay here, the people are great, but it's time to get moving.

MONDAY, MAY 28, 2018

Moxie Bald Mountain Shelter – 17.9 Miles

I shuttled to the trailhead at 9:00 a.m., started out slow after so many zeroes but soon picked up the pace and went fast through that gentle up-grade toward Moxie Bald Mountain. I forded both branches of the Piscataquis River without incident, kept the blackflies off this time with my new head net, found plenty of springs with beautiful, clean and cold water, arriving at Moxie Bald shelter late in the afternoon. A great day of hiking.

TUESDAY, MAY 29, 2018

Sterling Inn, Caratunk, Maine – 18.8 Miles

I slept well, just the rattle of mice getting into my stuff, along with two amorous squirrels that seemed to go at it all night. No moose, no bear, no other bother. Where are the moose, by the way? I usually see dozens by now, but I haven't seen one yet. Chris in Millinocket told me that a tick infestation was killing the calves. Apparently the ticks are able to survive the warmer winters, climate change and all. Deniers should come hike the Appalachian Trail and see for themselves.

I was on the way by 6:00 a.m., quick-timing the half mile toward my first climb of the day, Moxie Bald Mountain. This climb went reasonably fast despite its steepness and rock jumbles, and I reached that bald granite summit while the sun was still low and the wind was sharp and brisk. Gosh, what an all-encompassing view, and not a bug aloft in those crisp gusts.

Going down was a trial for my knees. The heat came up, and with it the bugs. My pace began to slow. To reach Pleasant Mountain you have to climb over a series of ridges that roll like granite waves between the peaks, up, up, up—gain the bare granite tops—down, down, down through tangled roots and boggy lows. A couple of smarmy blackflies snuck up my sleeve and bit my arm. The bastards. I'm scratching as I write this.

4.2 miles to Pleasant Mountains is nothing, I kept telling myself while again summiting something that wasn't Pleasant Mountain. Then a final steep grade, all in the trees, a drainage really, clotted with rounded rocks of various sizes, all washed clean by gushing rain water, poor footing, slow going.

When did I reach the peak? I was too tired to make note, 3:00 p.m. I think. There's a shelter not too far, where I bundled up wet and hypothermic last time, but Caratunk is only 6 miles farther. I couldn't make it in 2001 or 2008, but I would this time, that was a promise.

The trail keeps you up high for most of it. The leaves were crackling dry. No water on this side of the range. I ran out, a mistake that I repeat too often. I could have carried more water, but I was greedy to keep my pack weight down. It was as if I were back in the Mojave that time, doing the PCT and having run out of water yesterday. My throat was so dry that my voice was hoarse. My kidneys ached. I would come across a muddy seep and bend to dig a hole, hoping it would fill. No luck.

I slogged on over ridge after ridge, technically heading down but it never felt that way. I pushed on, stumbling sometimes, and at last descended into a hollow with a shallow stream. I dropped my pack, fell onto painful knees, thrust my water filter directly into the stream like a squat straw, and sucked in blessedly cool mouthfuls of water. Afterward I filled both containers, heavy but I wasn't going to run out of water again.

The last couple of miles are always the longest. Caratunk wasn't far, I could damn *hear* it, but it was still going to take a while to get there. Someone—for spite, perhaps—threw a PUD (pointless up and down) in the way just a mile or so from town, a tough upward slog that I made one shuffling foot at a time. I stumbled onto the highway at last, my feet feeling like aching bricks on that pavement. The little village of Caratunk was quiet. No one out, no cars, and the hostel, it seems, was not open. With no shelters nearby, my only choice was to walk back into the woods and roll up on the ground among the bugs and the biting chaos. I would have groaned if I'd had the energy.

Just then a car stopped across the way.

"Are you all right?" a woman asked.

"Uhgrawnuh," I answered hoarsely.

"Hop in. I'll take you to Sterling Inn."

Sterling Inn is a few miles down the road. I would never have made it on foot, and again in that weird juxtaposition, within an hour I was showered, drinking a local porter, eating a big burger along with mac and cheese, and thinking: 18.8 miles since this morning, a day faster than my 2008 hike, and I'm feeling pretty well.

WEDNESDAY, MAY 30, 2018

Sterling Inn, Caratunk, Maine – Zero

Sterling Inn is a lovingly restored nineteenth-century lodge run by a father, Eric, and his son, Zach. This place is so nice and comfortable that I have decided to zero today.

THURSDAY, MAY 31, 2018

West Carry Pond Shelter – 14 Miles

My hike from Caratunk started with a 9:00 a.m. canoe ferry across the Kennebec River, which is too fast and deep to safely ford. A hiker drowned just recently while trying. I hopped out on the opposite bank, shouldered my backpack, and set out under a clear, warm sky.

I met my first northbounder today, an athletic guy named Stitch, who was full of positive energy and looked as fresh as if he had just started his hike this morning, not 2000 miles ago.

I threw down at West Carry Pond shelter, where Dude and I sat out a rainstorm in 2001. I took a refreshing swim in the pond, then settled in for the night, alone with the chirps and screeches of evening.

FRIDAY, JUNE 1, 2018

Bigelow Col – 14.9 Miles

I set out early, needing to pull big miles in order to scale Bigelow Mountain, get over Avery Peak, then on through the col and over the Horn in order to reach Horns Pond shelter. Of course this is not how it went.

The hike started out nice—not too buggy, not too hot—and I made good time. The sky did not begin to fill until I started my climb some 11 miles later. Within minutes, the sky was almost black, loosing rain in cold, fat drops that drenched me at once. Rain guzzled from the bottom of my backpack. Icy rivulets ran down the back of my legs and into my shoes. Everything in my backpack is enclosed in ziplock bags so nothing got wet, but the weight of all of the water accumulating in my pack pulled at my shoulders, slowing me at a time when I needed to move fast.

The trail is steep here, with rock scrambles, exposed roots, and a well-trod path that was now flashing like an Arizona canyon after a thunderstorm. I had no choice but to push on through this since Horns Pond shelter, still a few climbs away, was closer than the last shelter behind me. I don't carry a tent, but it wouldn't have mattered anyway: the trail was too steep and rocky to pitch a tent even if I'd had one.

This went on for what seemed like hours, my pace slowed to barely ½ mile per hour. The rain never let up, so when I finally cleared the tree line onto that bald granite top I was fully exposed to the brunt of the storm. I could feel the wind stripping away my body heat despite the layers I was wearing; I cringed at the cold tracks running down my skin. The blazes appeared in and out of wind-driven clouds, while I leaned against my trekking poles to keep from blowing over.

I descended at last into the shelter of the opposing tree line, dropping into Bigelow Col, shivering as I went. There is no shelter in the col, although there should be. It was late in the day, a gray sky going grayer, and with three more miles over the Horn before I could reach shelter. I couldn't make it, not this time, not because of age but because of the ferocity of the storm. There is a caretaker hut in the col, but it was locked, the promise of shelter frustratingly close and yet inaccessible.

I uttered a few curses, slammed the lock, then cleared my head and made a plan. The hut's front porch was about eighteen inches wide, no roof over it but at least it offered a platform above the water sluicing over my feet. I found an old door leaning against the back of the hut, carried it around and propped it in place as a windbreak. I took out my emergency bivy, stuffed my sleeping bag into it, then slid in myself, still wet but at least warm. There's nothing to do now but wait for morning.

SATURDAY, JUNE 2, 2018

Stratton Motel, Stratton, Maine – 8.1 Miles

I awoke at 4:30 a.m., everything soaking wet. The rain had stopped, but the wind was cold and sharp. I got up in a hurry—no coffee—ate an energy bar, stuffed my sodden stuff into my sodden backpack, and got moving.

It took two hours to make the 3 miles to Horns Pond, so I had made the right decision last night: I would never have made it if I had pushed on.

At Horns Pond, I went into one of the two shelters just to get out of the wind, got my stove going and heated some ramen. The chemical broth from the flavor packet, something I would never eat off the trail, was extraordinarily cathartic. A ridge runner named Master Chipper appeared from the gloom and came in to talk with me. He is a young guy with his own pack of adventures, so we shared some warming stories while my core temperature rose.

Once my shivering stopped, I set out again for the final 5 miles down to the highway leading to the town of Stratton, where I had spent my 43rd birthday. It warmed as I descended—the sun even popped out a time or two. At the highway, I was picked up almost at once by a woman in a Mercedes SUV, who sped me to the Stratton Motel, still standing and with the three wooden bears out front as yet gripping their trekking poles. I stayed at the Stratton Motel during both my previous hikes, and was gratified to discover that the place was still open, although it has changed ownership at each of my visits. It was here in 2001 that the owners baked me a birthday cake; in 2008 when the new owner, Sue, presented me with the Kelty sleeping bag that I am still using; and now in 2018 as I sit with Baron, the caretaker, and study a roiling gray sky while shivering through gusts of chilling wind.

The weather is getting worse. I hope it clears out by tomorrow because I've got the Crocker Range and Sugarloaf Mountain next, and I'm not about to climb to those elevations when it's this wet and this cold.

SUNDAY, JUNE 3, 2018

Stratton Motel, Stratton, Maine – Zero

The hell with this, the weather is the worst, with clouds so low I can't even see the mountains, and with a freezing wind down here that cuts right through me. Imagine what it's like on top. I'm sitting it out, hoping for better weather tomorrow.

MONDAY, JUNE 4, 2018

Stratton Motel, Stratton, Maine – Zero

No improvement at all; if anything it's worse.

TUESDAY, JUNE 5, 2018

Stratton Motel, Stratton, Maine – Zero

Too many zeroes, but I still can't see the mountains, it's still raining, and it's still damn cold.

WEDNESDAY, JUNE 6, 2018

Spaulding Mountain Shelter – 13.5 Miles

The weather seemed to improve, and I was going stir crazy anyway, so I had Baron shuttle me back to the trail at 6:30 a.m.

 I wanted Poplar Ridge today, but I never saw the sun until I got here, and then only for a minute or two. I wasn't on the trail for an hour before the clouds socked in and the rain started. Cold, wet, slow going with the climbs, and no views at all. I stood under a fir tree to eat lunch, the only shelter from the rain I could find, but not much of a windbreak. I got here at 4:30 p.m., got the stove going, consulted my journal and discovered that I stayed in this same shelter on the same day in 2008! So all those zeroes have evened me up. I wonder how long I'll be able to match pace?

I'm settling in. It looks like a cold, quiet night ahead…

…but no. No sooner had I finished the last line than six nobos showed up, all wet and bedraggled, one a young woman who smelled worse than anything I have ever scented. Gag! They were making big miles, Mt. K in their sights. They'll get there in half the time it has taken me to get here, but that's the way it always is once you have your trail legs and are in that last third of your hike. My day for big miles will come, but it's still off a way yet.

So, anyway, for the first time ever in the state of Maine, I am sharing a shelter with nobos. They started their hikes in late January, snowshoeing through the Smokies and Grayson Highlands, ostensibly to get a head start on the northbound bubble. All they talked about was how cold it had been in the mountains down south, as if nothing else had occurred between there and here. They admitted to breaking into a wayside in Shenandoah for shelter when conditions had become really bad. The girl had gotten frostbite that day, she said. I remembered the day she spoke of. It had been four below zero at my farm, so imagine how much colder it was in the mountains.

Time to sleep. This ain't gonna be easy.

THURSDAY, JUNE 7, 2018

Hiker Hut, Sandy River, Maine – 19 Miles

Up at 4:30 a.m., on the trail by 5:30 a.m., and no, I didn't sleep well at all. I can still smell that girl (never got her trail name) on my clothes. Gack!

This day was no different than yesterday, cold, wet, rain, but I was determined to get over Saddleback Mountain and down to this new hostel called Hiker Hut, just .3 off the trail. I stopped in at Poplar Ridge shelter, near where Inchworm lost her life a few years ago, and where my stove blew up in 2001, then pushed and pushed through blowing clouds and spattering rain on Saddleback Mountain, marveling that in 2008 I had struggled through heat and humidity. I finally reached the road to Rangeley, then took the short .3-mile walk to the right to reach Hiker Hut.

It was about 6:30 p.m., gloomy because of the low ceiling, the chill just a constant by this point, but my spirits lifted the moment I stepped into what felt like more of a tranquil enclave than a hiker hostel. There were flowerbeds and a gurgling stream, bird feeders and rustic hand-built cabins. The place felt like peace.

The proprietor, Steve, was on a ladder securing some shingles on the main bunkhouse.

"Hey, there," he hollered down. "What can I do for you?"

"Hot shower, hot food, cold beer," I answered wearily."

"Okay, then," he said. "Let's go."

In the next moment we were in his old red truck rattling into Rangeley, where I had a shower at the local gym and everything else at the local pub. By the time the sun had set, I was sated, comfortable, and already forgetting how difficult the last couple of days had been.

FRIDAY, JUNE 8, 2018

Hiker Hut, Sandy River, Maine – Zero

I have an embarrassing accumulation of zeroes going on, but today is my 60th birthday so I'm entitled. No other hikers are here, and the weather is suddenly absolutely perfect: polar blue, golden sun, and embracing warmth.

I like Steve. He's my age, a Tibetan Buddhist, and has his own wealth of stories. Now I understand the serenity of this place, it's the Tibetan motif. Hiker Hut is off the grid, Steve uses solar panels to charge phones and such. The heater he put in the bunkhouse last night ran on batteries. I cannot express how well I slept.

I had a notion—it was just something about the place that felt right. I thought some of Freewind's ashes belonged in a place like this, so I broached the subject with Steve, not sure how he would react. For all I know, Buddhists are not down for that kind of thing, but Steve became very somber, very respectful.

Hiker Hut

"I'd be honored," he said, taking it one step further. "I'm planting dahlias in the garden in front of the bunkhouse today. We'll put his ashes there so that every hiker who comes here will know Freewind."

I was astounded, but also touched.

About mid-afternoon, the sky glorious, Steve's friend Kathy arrived with the flowers. She dug the holes then stood aside as Steve chanted and rang a Tibetan bell, all to the sweet smell of incense. When he was finished, I sprinkled Freewind's ashes into the holes and then Kathy put in the flowers. My eyes misted. It was an emotional experience.

Later that evening, Steve cooked me a birthday dinner of spaghetti with big meatballs, which I downed ravenously. Afterward we sat around a campfire in the lowering light, drank a few beers and watched fish leap in the stream.

What a great birthday.

SATURDAY, JUNE 9, 2018

Bemis Mountain Shelter – 18 Miles

I moved well today, made good time and felt strong. Arrived here at 6:30 p.m. Sharing the shelter with nobos Peanut Butter and his girlfriend Jelly. Jelly lost her prescription glasses in Mahoosuc Notch, so I'm going to look for them when I get there. If I find them, I'll mail them to Shaw's.

SUNDAY, JUNE 10, 2018

Pine Ellis Hostel, Andover, Maine – 8.7 Miles

I have stayed at Pine Ellis Hostel in Andover twice before, so when I reached South Arm Road I held out my thumb for a hitch into town. It was still relatively early—I could have made even more miles—but I really wanted to reconnect with the place, to see if Ilene and David were still there and in good health. Both were still there, keeping the place going. I recognized Ilene right away, ten years older but still spry. I didn't recognize David at first, which led to an awkward moment, but then I could see through the decade to the man I had met in 2008 and it all came back to me.

Just relaxing now. It's good to be here again.

MONDAY, JUNE 11, 2018

Pine Ellis Hostel, Andover, Maine – 10.1 Miles

David shuttled me back to the trailhead this morning, and then I took off, hiking strong. I had planned an 18-mile hike over Bald Pate Mountain to the shelter on the other side, was moving out fast and well, feeling good in the great weather, when after 10 miles I came to B-Hill Road. This is another road leading into Andover, but for me it was just a crossing. I had been to Pine Ellis, I didn't need to go back. It was early enough, and I looked forward to summiting Bald Pate in good weather.

And then this happened...

Perhaps the strangest, most coincidental thing occurred the very moment I set my right foot on the pavement. My left foot was still on the duff of the trail, both trekking poles still embedded in leaves and dirt, my eyes searching across the road for the next white blaze, when a pickup truck screeched to a halt right then and a guy leaned out his window and hollered, "You heading to Pine Ellis?"

I was a bit bewildered. It took me a moment to process the suddenness of this, the sheer incongruity of it. I found myself nodding in a daze. "Yes," I said with certainty. "Yes I am."

"Well hop in, then," he said.

His name was Peter and his dog was named Jack. Peter had a summer cabin nearby, which is why he was on that isolated road. Jack sat placidly in my lap as we went the nine miles or so into Andover. Peter dropped me at an intersection near Pine Ellis, and so not even noon yet, I walked in and said hi to Ilene and David.

"Why are you back?" they asked me in unison. I explained the bizarre circumstances to them, the pure serendipity of it. Ilene pondered this. "You're meant to do something," she said.

I'm not a believer in preordained stuff, in destiny and such, but this was a weird thing. I'm glad I followed the signs just the same, although I have yet to connect them with a reason why. Who knows where time will roll? Sometimes you just have to go with the mystery, and things will fall where they will.

TUESDAY, JUNE 12, 2018

Baldpate Shelter – 8 Miles

Short miles today because if I had pushed on I would have had to stay at Speck Pond shelter, which is an AMC (Appalachian Mountain Club) site so of course you have to pay, which is anathema to a thru-hiker. By doing short miles, I can pass up Speck and make it to Full Goose shelter on the other side of Mahoosuc Notch or else Carlo Col shelter 4 miles farther on, and then after that I can make it to Gorham.

I didn't leave Pine Ellis until after noon. A southbounder showed up, Wisecrack, a young, determined guy racing down the trail in order to get back to his girlfriend as soon as possible. I guess they're a thru-hiking duo, and since she has already thru-hiked the AT, he feels he needs to get it done as well. He's taking a zero today, so he'll be two days behind me. I'm sure we'll meet up again in Gorham.

It's nice to be alone in shelter again.

WEDNESDAY, JUNE 13, 2018

Full Goose Shelter – 12 Miles

On the trail by 6:00 a.m., made quick time to Grafton Notch, the end of MATC country and the beginning of AMC country. Check your wallets. It took three hours to get over Speck Mountain. The views were great and it wasn't too buggy. I met a nobo on the way down, Frank, a girl, hiking solo and with the spirit of a cheerleading team.

Mahoosuc Notch killed me this time. The blazing is really bad now, and I kept shunting off the trail and up the sides of the notch. Very frustrating. I didn't find Jelly's glasses.

Made Full Goose by 4:30 p.m. and decided not to push on to Carlo Col shelter, which I did on both my previous hikes. It's not that I'm tired, just that this is a nice place to relax, good breeze, not buggy. There are three section hikers here, good conversation.

THURSDAY, JUNE 14, 2018

Gorham, New Hampshire – 21.7 Miles

I set out at 5:30 a.m., the other hikers curled in their bags and snoring away. Three hours to the New Hampshire state line. I stopped for photos, no one else around. I was here on the same day in 2008, thought I would try to stage my photos so that they would be identical to ten years ago, but to my disappointment the signs have been replaced. The old, hand painted *Welcome to Maine, The Way Life Should*

Be sign is gone, along with the old *New Hampshire, ~~Live~~ Hike Free or Die* sign. Both have been replaced with modern AMC signs. It's sad to lose that authenticity.

Soon the sky closed in, gray through the trees. The rain started while I was climbing that slippery, boulder-strewn trail up Mt. Success, but lightly on and off, as if the rain were trying to decide what it wanted to do. Still spattering when I reached the summit, the sky getting blacker, the wind colder, I found myself racing for Gentian Pond shelter, desperate to get under cover before everything became soaked, like a repeat of the Bigelows.

I reached Gentian Pond shelter at 12:45 p.m., ducked in, and just then the sky unloaded a hard slanting rain with such force that it drove a chill gust of displaced air into the shelter. I still had 12 miles to go before I could reach the comfort and sanctuary of Gorham, and this over a couple of mountains that would slow my progress even on a nice day. I watched the rain, pondered, got cold, then surrendered to the last of my dry clothes. By 1:45 p.m., the rain began to slack. I committed myself, stepped into the wet, and made for Gorham. This was it: if the weather didn't improve I would be wet to the core and with nothing else dry to wear. 12 miles—I could do it. I would do it. I had no choice.

The rain eventually stopped, although I was as wet as I knew I would be. I started my descent of Mt. Hayes as the sun set, sprinting down those interminable last 3.5 miles to Gorham in what seemed to be a race with the night. The blazing was poor in this section, shunting me onto social trails a few times. I cursed my way back onto the AT each time, glancing at my watch to note the time wasted. The mosquitoes came out in swarms. I could see the lights of Gorham across the river and through the trees, but I still had a mile or more to go.

Damn, no blazes! And damn the mosquitoes. I came out onto Hogan Road in the twilight, couldn't remember if I needed to go left or right, no blazes, I went the wrong way, figured it out, went the other way, caught North Road at last, turned right, dark, mosquitoes, wet, tired, there's Rattle River Lodge and Hostel, right on the trail, no need to hitch into Gorham. It wasn't in business last time, but 2008 doesn't matter anymore, only now. I went around back to the hostel entrance, dripping, cold, went inside, and stood—dumbstruck.

The place was full of northbounders, 100% full, not even room to sleep on the floor!

I wilted in place. Night had taken over beyond the door. I had nothing left. Erik, the owner, felt pity. He shuttled me to a motel in town, where I showered, ate, and sipped a celebratory single-malt. Once again, to the best of my knowledge, I'm the first southbounder to finish the state of Maine.

Now I've got the White Mountains to deal with.

FRIDAY, JUNE 15, 2018

Rattle River Hostel, Gorham, New Hampshire – Zero

The nobos cleared out of the hostel this morning, so I caught a ride back. The hostel is a lot cheaper than the motel. I tried to imagine that big bubble of northbounders moving across Maine. By this point they would all be hiking strong, likely to still be together at K. They will fill every shelter, every hostel. I've never seen anything like it this far north.

Another damn zero, but I got in too late to do any resupply. I also have to dry out my equipment and get myself ready for the White Mountains.

Wisecrack showed up today. He made the hike from Bald Pate to Gentian Pond in one pull! Man, he's a strong hiker.

SATURDAY, JUNE 16, 2018

Rattle River Hostel, Gorham, New Hampshire – Zero

Yeah, another zero. I felt fatigued this morning, and I have the Wildcats to do next, a tough section that I want to do in one pull. I've never achieved that before, so another day of rest is worth it.

SUNDAY, JUNE 17, 2018

Pinkham Notch – 21.1 Miles

When I hiked the Wildcats in 2008, the weather was cold and wet, the going as slow as you can imagine. I only made it as far as Carter Notch Hut that day, drug in cold, teeth chattering, and desperate for hot coffee. This time the weather was incredible, clear and warm but not too hot. What a contrast!

I started hiking at 4:30 a.m., wanting to be sure I had plenty of time to get to Pinkham Notch. Although the hostel is run by former thru-hikers, nobody seemed to know if the Wildcats could be done by a southbounder in one day. My previous experience doesn't help because the conditions are so different now. I learned that Rattle River Hostel runs a shuttle to Pinkham Notch at 5:00 p.m. every day, which was another incentive for me. If I could reach Pinkham Notch in time, I could return here tonight and not have to pay to stay in an AMC facility.

It was a novelty to just step out of the hostel and onto the trail. I flew through those first 5 miles, the easy upgrade that follows the river. The blazing was bad in this section, too. It was sometimes hard to find the trail, especially in the dark, but in the end it didn't cost me too much time.

The sun came up as I went over Mt. Moriah. Gosh, what an exhilarating view! Again on North Carter Mountain. I slowed through this, it was just too beautiful. These are views I had never seen before since it had been overcast and raining on both my previous hikes. On Mt. Hight, I had a 360° view of the surrounding mountains, including across the valley at Mt. Washington, which I will climb tomorrow if all goes well. There are some incredible views on the Appalachian Trail, but I think the view from Mt. Hight has to be among the best of them.

I reached Carter Notch Hut at 2:30 p.m., didn't go in, just sat by the lake, reveling in the sun. What a dream of a hike it had become!

The next couple of hours went quickly despite the climbs. I went over both Wildcat peaks, just trying to catch my breath from the views, then made the steep, rocky descent into Pinkham Notch.

I reached the AMC visitor center with time to spare, sat on the stone wall along the parking area and waited for the shuttle back to Gorham. There were two southbounders at the hostel when I got back, Mr. Hiker, a young, taciturn guy from North Carolina, and Whip, whom I didn't recognize until he told me that he was the Canadian guy I met when I climbed K! It turns out that he and his wife had turned back after they encountered some rocks they couldn't climb over, and then the next morning they hiked up the Abol Trail instead.

It was great to see Whip, great that he stuck with it. What an incredible day.

MONDAY, JUNE 18, 2018

Rattle River Hostel, Gorham, New Hampshire – Zero

Are you kidding? A storm moved in overnight. The trail to Mt. Washington is closed. No choice but to sit it out.

TUESDAY, JUNE 19, 2018

Lakes of the Clouds Hut – 15 Miles

Storm? What storm? Today the sky is clear again, warm in the notch. It's 7:30 a.m., time to get moving.

I started out fast, climbing through the woods, but slowed on the rocks when I cleared the tree line. Mt. Madison was tough as always, the footing poor and the wind howling. I stopped in at Mt. Madison Hut for water, but didn't linger because I wanted to make Lakes of the Clouds Hut while it was still light. At some point—I'm not exactly sure where—I rounded a peak and stepped into a gust that just about blew me off the mountain. I do not exaggerate. And the wind was cold. If not for the bright sun and the albedo off the rocks, I would probably have gone hypothermic.

I reached the Mt. Washington visitor center at 5:00 p.m., just as it was about to close up, scored a coffee and some sugary calories, and took shelter from the pummeling wind for a few minutes. Even indoors, the wind seemed to still be roaring in my ears. I was told that the gusts were in excess of 90 mph, and I believe it. On a ridgeline near Mt. Washington, I leaned into the wind over the precipice and was held aloft, like flying. Of course, if the wind had suddenly died off I would have been a goner. I wanted to leave some of Freewind's ashes on Mt. Washington, but I was too afraid to open the container, fearing the wind would take them all.

Made the last mile and a half or so to Lakes of the Clouds Hut quickly. About ten northbounders were already there, but the croo offered me a work-for-stay anyway. The Lakes of the Clouds croo have always been the best. I looked down in the Dungeon for old time's sake. It looks as if it has been renovated. I guess so, since they charge money to stay down there now.

We thru-hikers all waited as a group while the paying guests ate dinner. I took down the 2001 and 2008 trail registers to find my entries, which gave me a deep sense of accomplishment and connection. If not for yesterday's storm, I would have been here on the same day as 2008.

Once the paying guests were done with dinner, we thru-hikers got to eat all the leftovers. Man, I was hungry. We ate potatoes and pie, roast beef and some sausage. Between all of us, we scraped the bottom of every pan. This works out well for the croo because otherwise they would have to hike all of the leftovers out, for composting down in the notch. There are no roads to the hut, no cars and trucks, so everything that comes in and out of the huts is carried up and down the trail in pack frames by the croo.

Later, I washed dishes with a German nobo named Conan. I also met a South African nobo named Metric. At lights out, we all sacked out on the floor in the dining area. We used to sleep on the tables, but someone probably figured out that this isn't too hygienic.

WEDNESDAY, JUNE 20, 2018

Crawford Notch – 11 Miles

Short miles today, but you have to stage your transit of the Whites or else you can wind up on an exposed ridge with no shelter when the sun sets. I've known thru-hikers who will do the Whites in the dark. I'm not one of them.

The weather was great again, chilly in the morning. I was on the trail by 6:00 a.m. and made good time over Mts. Jackson and Webster. The descent into Crawford Notch was tough as always, hand-over-hand for a good part of it. Difficult enough for a southbounder going down, Crawford Notch is, in my opinion, one of the toughest climbs for a northbounder.

I hiked into the notch at 2:00 p.m., already knowing that I was not going to climb up the other side to Ethan Pond, but perhaps I should have. In my memory there was a campground in this notch, but if so it is gone now. I had to hitch to the AMC Center and pay too much for a bunk. So my goal to get through AMC country without spending money is blown, but at least the food was good and plentiful. Also, no other hikers here. A quiet night.

THURSDAY, JUNE 21, 2018

Galehead Hut – 14.7 Miles

Got an early hitch to the trailhead, made the climb in good time, and had a great hike in great weather. Views, views, views, especially on South Twin Mountain. Man, if I lived in the area I would be up here all the time.

I was pushing for Garfield Ridge shelter, same hike I made the previous two times, but when I stopped in at Galehead Hut at 4:15 p.m. for water, the hut master, Amber, offered me a work-for-stay. So why not? It's worth it for the food if nothing else, plus this is a great croo.

There's a northbounder here named Dude. I got a laugh out of that. He laughed too when I told him about my southbounder pal Dude from 2001.

FRIDAY, JUNE 22, 2018

Franconia Notch – 13 Miles

Woke up early. My job this morning is to sweep out the dining area, then I can be on my way.

Hiking by 6:00 a.m., I moved out fast to Garfield Ridge, where I stopped in to sign the register. The old cabin is gone, replaced by a new Gentian Pond-style double decker. I miss that cabin, where Jake Brake and Willow have their night of passion in my novel, and where I was awoken by a curious moose in 2008. I never took photos of the old cabin, so now it exists only in my memory. (And I still haven't seen a moose, or even fresh droppings!)

I met the caretaker, Rachel, who asked me to carry a message to her boyfriend, Ryan, who is the caretaker at Liberty Springs Campground about 8 miles farther on. This wound up being fortuitous.

Soon I was climbing up Mt. Lafayette, which was tiring but gorgeous in the perfect weather. The trail was crowded with day hikers, who congregated in the trail, stopping to take their selfies and generally impeding progress. On Mt. Lafayette, I pushed through the maddening crowd and went off trail around a peak to find a quiet nook where I could eat lunch and take in the view.

Franconia Ridge was mostly clear of day hikers, so I could pause at my leisure to take in those breathtaking views. At Liberty Springs, I took the side trail down to the campground to deliver Rachel's message. This was a steep descent of about a half a mile, which had me questioning the wisdom of accepting Rachel's request since I would now have to climb back out of this. But then, after delivering the message, I discovered that the trail to the campground was the AT! The blazing had been so bad that if I hadn't gone down to deliver Rachel's message I would have continued onto a side trail to who knows where.

It took a couple more hours to reach the bike path to the Flume Visitor Center, which is .9 off the AT, where I learned that all the hostels were full because of Brewfest. I finally found a vacancy at a motel, farther from the trail than I wanted but at least it's close to restaurants and resupply. The owner is going to shuttle me back in the morning.

SATURDAY, JUNE 23, 2018

Eliza Brook Shelter – 8.8 Miles

I couldn't get a ride to the trailhead until 9:00 a.m., the downside of staying so far from the trail. This was not a hard section, though. I made great time and would have pushed on to Kinsman Notch if the sky hadn't abruptly closed in. Suddenly it was raining and cold, and I mean cold enough to get my attention. I reached Eliza Brook shelter just in time to avoid the worst of it, just my shoes and socks were soaked. Pools formed outside the shelter, and the trail was sluicing like a stream.

This is a newer shelter, built in 2010 and all by hand, with wooden pegs instead of nails. The trail volunteers did a great job on it, and thru-hikers so far have not carved it up with graffiti and such. I had the place to myself, figuring it would stay that way because other thru-hikers would surely be hunkering down somewhere.

I held on to that thought as a pair of section hikers came in, a young couple who splashed around in the rain looking for a place to pitch their tent. They finally came to stand under the eave to get out of the rain. I told them to come on into the shelter, there was plenty of room. I don't snore, I reassured them, and I was almost certain that no one else would be stopping here.

They took me up on that, and now I feel bad about it because no sooner had they gotten their gear unpacked and themselves settled in than a dozen or more nobos showed up, so many that we couldn't get them all in the shelter. Tents started popping up in the rain, three, four, five, six, more around the corner and out back. Hikers kept coming in, standing under the eave and out of the rain while they figured out what to do.

Inside the shelter, I was pushed up against one wall, while the section-hiking couple was pushed against the other. They shot a look of misery at me across unwashed bodies that were lined up like matches in a box. I mouthed, "I'm sorry," at them. I could tell that they now wished beyond anything that they had set up their tent instead, but for whatever reason they stayed put now.

The guy lying next to me is a dick, bragging about his miles and how we sobos haven't done anything yet. He keeps encroaching into my space—and all I really have is the width of my sleeping bag—moving my gear to make room for his. I want to tell the guy off, but since I'm stuck shoulder-to-shoulder with him for the next however many hours, I'm biting my tongue.

I have never experienced this kind of crowding. How many hikers are on the trail now, two, three, four times more than my previous hikes? I don't carry a tent because I've never had to. Why carry the weight, this is what the shelters are for. I learned this in 2001, when I eventually shipped my tent home because I simply hadn't needed it. But now—if this keeps up I'll need to change my philosophy, at least until I clear the northbounder bubble in New Jersey.

Anyway, it turns out that one of the bodies toward the middle of the shelter belongs to a southbounder named Chipmunk, a youngish guy with a floppy hat, colorful shorts, and bicycle arm warmers. I can't really talk to him, though, because of all the bodies in between.

It's going to be a long, smelly night.

SUNDAY, JUNE 24, 2018

Kinsman Notch - 7.5 Miles

Man, that was as nasty a night as I have ever spent in shelter. I thought the dick next to me was unzipping his bag at daybreak, but no, that's not what that sound was. Gack!

No fanfare this morning, not even coffee. I just downed an energy bar, and at 5:45 a.m. got the hell out of there.

It wasn't raining, but the woods were cold, foggy, and generally uninspiring. I was hiking fast, soon catching up to Chipmunk, who had slipped out a few minutes ahead of me. In the tangle of bodies, I hadn't noticed him leaving. It turns out that he is trying to speed-hike the trail in ninety days, which means I will never see him again, or Wisecrack, who Chipmunk says is at least two days ahead now. I think these guys might have a competition going on.

We hiked together into Kinsman Notch, where I turned left to the parking lot to wait for my shuttle to the motel. We fist-bumped, then Chipmunk plunged back into the dripping, fog-enclosed woods to begin his ascent of Mt. Moosilauke. That's a slippery climb, across bare granite in places, which I would not want to make in this weather. I hope he'll be all right.

While waiting for a hitch into town, I met a father-daughter team named Grits and Tree Line. They're flip-floppers, meaning they started their hike at Harpers Ferry. After they summit K, they will fly down to Georgia and then hike from Springer to Harpers Ferry. Apparently the ATC (Appalachian Trail Conservancy) encourages flip-flop hikes as a way to thin that northbounder bubble. So things really have gotten crowded on the trail these past few years. I had no idea. It's possible that I'll see Grits and Tree Line again on my way south, maybe in Virginia. That would be a real novelty, although a flip-flop hike is not something that would ever interest me.

Now I'm at a brewpub in Lincoln enjoying a nice porter. This bacon cheeseburger is nice, too.

MONDAY, JUNE 25, 2018

Glencliff, New Hampshire – 9.3 Miles

The weather was clearing as I climbed Mt. Moosilauke, the rocks still slippery, but no rain. Still cold, though.

I took it slow on that steep, slick section along the waterfall. Without the rebar handholds drilled into the granite, I don't think it would be possible to climb this in wet conditions. Northbounders

Climb up Mt. Moosilauke

have to come down this, which I think is even more dangerous. Rumor has it someone slipped off of here since my last hike, careened down like a toboggan in a chute. Not a survivable fall.

The sun finally broke through when I cleared the trees, the clouds lifting high enough to give me some great views. I could look back toward Mt. Washington and marvel at the peaks I had climbed, and ahead to Mt. Cube and the peaks yet to come, although these are not nearly as high. The wind was gusting hard and cold, so I took shelter behind some rocks, ate lunch, and then pushed on.

It took me five and a half hours to get over Mt. Moosilauke. I was going to continue on to the Ore Hill shelter, but learned that it is gone, burned down by a careless hiker or amorous locals, depending upon whom you ask. So instead I'm staying at the Hikers Welcome Hostel just off the trail. I've stayed here before. The old Windows XP computer on the desk over there looks to be the same one I used to post field notes ten years ago. It's covered in dust, but I'm told it still works.

Because of smart phones, hardly anyone uses computers on the trail anymore. In 2001, cell phones on the trail were rare. Bringing a phone onto the trail, we thought, was a strange thing to do. By

2008 though, everybody had cell phones—and now everybody carries a smart phone. I've seen hikers thumbing them as they hiked, picking up bars on the mountaintops, checking their apps, Facetiming as they go, opening apps that provide the latest trail info down to the hour. Some hikers have GPS trackers attached to their backpacks, with panic buttons in case they get into trouble, and insurance policies that will pluck them out of the woods in case of mishap. What happened to self-reliance, to disconnecting from everyday life? Why are these people hiking?

Oh well, the White Mountains are behind me now. I have hiked 400 miles, lost about fifteen pounds, and have never felt better. So now I think I'll sit down at that old computer and post some field notes.

TUESDAY, JUNE 26, 2018

Fire Warden's Cabin – 20.1 Miles

It was cold this morning but great weather otherwise. On the trail at 6:30 a.m.

I met the Omelet Man at 11:00 a.m. He had a propane stove and fridge set up in a large open tent right off the trail, with a stack of egg crates as high as my shoulders. The Omelet Man offers free omelets, cookies, and juice to hikers. He made me a four-egg omelet that was so large and packed with goodies that I could barely finish it. I hung around until noon, drinking juice and talking with the Omelet Man. He's an interesting guy, retired and loves the trail. He's been doing this for a few years, he said. He's the first trail angel I've met on this hike.

I took off at noon when a squad of nobos showed up. The hike went well until I climbed Mt. Cube, which drained me despite the excellent views. I went past Hexacuba shelter without going in, since nobos told me that the water source was dry. I stopped in at this shelter in 2001. It is a unique, six-sided shelter designed by an architecture class at Dartmouth College. I'm in Dartmouth Outing Club country now. Many of the shelters and privies in this section are known for their originality.

My energy flattened on Smart Mountain. I'm just beat, despite the omelet and the good weather. Don't know why. A young woman jogging on the trail came up quietly behind me as I approached the Fire Warden's Cabin. I was so startled that I almost stabbed her with my poles, thinking she was a bear or other varmint. She didn't even apologize, just wordlessly shouldered past me and kept going. What a dick.

I'm alone in shelter, and look forward to a quiet night. It was here in 2008 that I came up with the idea for my novel, *The Appalachian*.

WEDNESDAY, JUNE 27, 2018

Tigger's Treehouse – 17.5 Miles

A nobo named Miles came in last night, a cocky guy trying to finish the trail in 100 days. I stayed up until hiker midnight (9:00 p.m.) coaching him on conditions in the Whites and in the state of Maine. He appreciated the information, and I scored some energy bars as a result.

I was weary and lethargic again today. Holt's Ledge and Moose Mountain took it out of me, even though these are not hard climbs. I reached Etna, New Hampshire at 4:00 p.m., and got a shuttle to Tigger's Treehouse, a little hostel run by a woman named Karen. I also stayed here in 2008. Karen didn't remember me, but I remembered her.

There is a father-daughter team of flip-floppers here. His name is Hoagie, and her name is Sniffles. Although I would not want to do a flip-flop hike, I envy these father-daughter teams. Their experiences must be irreplaceable.

It has started to rain.

THURSDAY, JUNE 28, 2018

Norwich, Vermont – 7.3 Miles

Karen shuttled me in the rain to the trailhead at 7:00 a.m. It rained continuously as I hiked into Hanover, still raining as I came out of the woods behind the Dartmouth ball field and then followed the sidewalk through town. There used to be a frat house in Hanover that allowed hikers to stay in the basement, but not anymore. Now there is no lodging for hikers in Hanover. I also noticed fewer blazes. While Hanover is a small town and easy to hike across, it is still disorienting to come out of the woods and suddenly be among traffic and people, especially in the rain. So the blazes really help. They used to appear on every lamppost, even on the sidewalk itself. This time, I found myself pausing and searching at each intersection, not sure which way to go. Perhaps Hanover is no longer the friendly hiker town it once was.

I crossed the bridge over the Connecticut River—still raining—and hiked into Vermont, my third state. Nobos passed me going the other way, all dripping, hair plastered to faces, and as sodden as I. Even though it was early yet, I needed resupply and out of this rain, so I took a room at the historic Norwich Inn, just a block off the trail. Even though I was dripping on the hardwood floor of their lobby, the staff members were polite and helpful, hiker friendly, as we say. That sense of welcome is deeply gratifying after the rigors of the trail.

There's a brewpub in the Inn. I'm heading straight there after a shower.

FRIDAY, JUNE 29, 2018

Vermont Route 12 – 21.7 Miles

Woke up early, but it took a while for the hotel to wake up. Packed, paced, drank coffee, and then it was finally 7:30 a.m. and breakfast. I met Iceager at breakfast, a 63-year-old flip-flopper. Interesting guy.

Just like that, hot weather is coming, so I waited until 8:30 a.m. for the post office to open. Mailed off my cold weather stuff—I won't need it again until maybe Tennessee—and got hiking at 9:00 a.m.

Man, it suddenly got hot. Hiking shirtless for the first time, I went fast, fast, fast over the easier terrain. Met some trail angels in West Hartford who were handing out hot dogs and Pepsis. I drank one Pepsi—I'm trying to stay away from sugary drinks on this hike—but ate a lot of hot dogs.

I began to wear down late in the day, the heat taking a toll. Heat? Didn't have the sand to make Winturri shelter, so hitched out at Route 12 and got a room.

SATURDAY, JUNE 30, 2018

Stoney Brook Shelter – 13.7 Miles

My knees and ankles ache for some reason. Not strong today, feel wiped out. Muchos nobos on the trail. I lost count.

I pulled in here early, and then the shelter filled up with nobos. A good group, though. One, a young, vaguely Asian-looking woman named Sail, is a real polymath. We discussed particle physics—yes, *particle physics*. Higgs Boson and such. The other hikers were incredulous as this went on. Sail says she is a sometimes teacher, sometimes hand on sailing boats, hence her trail name. She started her hike in Alabama and plans to continue onto the International AT after she climbs Mt. Katahdin. An additional talent, she played an Indian flute as the sun set.

A nobo named Ridge offered some trail wisdom that I simply had to write down: *When you get into shelter, you're hungry, you're tired, and you probably need to shit—* Blunt but true, Ridge.

SUNDAY, JULY 1, 2018

Inn at Long Trail – 8.6 Miles

The humidity is really high today. Maybe this is why I've been so weary. It doesn't feel that hot, but sweat is coming out of me in rivulets. I decided to take a nero (near zero) into the Inn at Long Trail for old time's sake. I came in here with Dude in 2001. The trail was relocated later that year, so I wound up completely bypassing the place in 2008. It had been a trail tradition for decades.

This time I took the blue blaze down, which I don't consider cheating because, prior to 2001, this blue blaze was the Appalachian Trail.

It's good to be back. I remembered Hoagie, gruff as always, and of course McGrath's Irish Pub. I've now had several bowls of stew, twice that many Long Trail Ales, and I'm feeling as cool as this bottle in my hand.

MONDAY, JULY 2, 2018

Vermont Route 103 – 20.1 Miles

Climbed the blue blaze up to Pico at 8:00 a.m. Feeling much better today. Arrived at Clarendon shelter at 4:00 p.m., but decided to push on and make some more miles. Just as I stepped onto Route 103 a mile later, the bus to Rutland serendipitously pulled up. The driver looked at me and shrugged the question. The bus was otherwise empty. Shaking my head and laughing inwardly, I followed the signs once more and climbed aboard. When I told the driver that I didn't have any cash, just a debit card, he, without hesitation, reached into his pocket and fed the cash box for me. Wow.

Now I'm at the Yellow Deli Hostel in Rutland, the place all the nobos have been talking about. There is some kind of religious element to the place, but no one has tried to preach to me. Otherwise they have a nice setup, with the bunkroom upstairs, and a bakery downstairs. Mr. Hiker is here! I haven't seen him since Gorham. He came in from Sherburne Gap, so he's a day behind me.

Now to go find some food.

TUESDAY, JULY 3, 2018

Lost Pond Shelter – 17.6 Miles

Spent a good night at Yellow Deli, had coffee and baked goods downstairs, talked some more with Mr. Hiker, then caught my bus back to the trailhead at 7:05 a.m.

At the Route 140 trailhead parking, I met a trail angel named Fresh Ground, who was serving hot dogs, chicken pasta, and juice to the hikers. Of course I stopped in for a while. Fresh Ground told me that, living in his van, he starts each season down south and parallels the northbounders as they journey toward Mt. K, parking at the trailheads and putting out the food. He said he'd been doing this for about eight years. He seems too young to be retired, but I didn't press him for how he can afford it all.

Fresh Ground

We visited for an hour, and then I pushed on into some rocky climbs. A thru-hiking family called The Family passed me in a long procession, kids aged from early teenagers to single digits, one of them carrying a toddler on her shoulders. The parents brought up the rear, looking much too young to have made so many children. We stopped to talk for a while, but as the kids were getting too far ahead, we had to keep our conversation short. Considering that The Family had already hiked more than 1700 miles, everybody looked to be in great shape.

The heat came up, slowing me, everything soaked with sweat. There were no hikers at Lost Pond shelter, so I stripped, bathed in the stream, then washed everything.

I feel better, and as the sun sets, no other hikers have come in. It's much cooler now, and it looks as if I have the shelter to myself. This is going to be a great night.

WEDNESDAY, INDEPENDENCE DAY, 2018

Vermont Route 11 – 14.8 Miles

Woke up to a cooler morning. Sunrise is noticeably later now.

Got out at 6:00 a.m., feeling well and making good time. This lasted until I climbed Bromley Mountain and the heat returned. Still, I was doing okay. I decided to skip Manchester Center this time and make more miles, but when I stepped out onto Route 11 a local police officer pulled up in his squad car and offered me a ride into town. What the heck is going on with all of these serendipitous, spur of the moment rides? So I followed the signs once more to see where they would lead, and wound up at Green Mountain Hostel, which is owned by a previous thru-hiker named Flashback. It's a nice place.

Flashback shuttled me into town, where I was able resupply and get my trekking pole tips replaced. I bent them during the climbs yesterday, when I tripped and went down hard. Leki poles have a lifetime warranty, which The Mountain Goat outfitters honored. Nice shop, good people. Later, at the hostel, I was able to wash out my smelly backpack and dry it in the sun. Whew, glad I got that done!

Now fireworks are popping off out there somewhere. We can see them from the hostel. A nice show.

THURSDAY, JULY 5, 2018

Story Spring Shelter – 21.1 Miles

Had a great day of hiking. On the trail by 7:00 a.m. Good weather.

Climbed Stratton Mountain, stopping in at that gorgeous piped spring on top. Cold spring water is the best. I went down the other side, weather still awesome, reaching Story Spring shelter at 5:00 p.m. There's a Connecticut Trail Club volunteer here named Jim. He's out for a section hike, but he thru-hiked the AT in 1980. What fascinating stories he has of the Appalachian Trail of that era. The trail was a lot wilder then, the waning days of which I got a sense of during my 2001 hike. The equipment they used is all terribly heavy by today's standards: external frame backpacks, cotton clothing, Coleman sleeping bags, and canvas tents. Jim says they seldom treated water, just drank it straight from the source. And, he added, he never knew anyone to get sick.

The shelter has filled up, all of us shoulder-to-shoulder, but it's a good, respectful group. Lots of great stories.

FRIDAY, JULY 6, 2018

Bennington, Vermont – 19 Miles

I was up at 4:00 a.m., having slept surprisingly well despite the crowding, but no sooner did I have my backpack ready to go than the sky opened up with thunder and rain and the crackle of lightening. I sat out the deluge for two hours, then at 6:00 a.m. finally stepped out into it.

The trail was muddy and slippery, the rain incessant. I pushed on through the downpour, the hours running together, the trail a running stream. At least it was a warm rain. I eventually stripped down to just my Spandex shorts and a backpack covered with a trash bag.

I stopped at every shelter along the way just to get out of the torrent for a while, meeting nobos in the same miserable condition as I. And then without notice I popped out into a power line clearing, the sun miraculously appeared, and I met a section hiker named Emma, who hiked the final two miles with me.

We met some trail angels at the trailhead who were giving out juice, chips, and other snacks. We visited and ate, and then Emma went off to find a place to camp while I hitched into Bennington. I got in too late to pick up my mail drop at the post office, so took a room at a hiker friendly place called Catamount Motel, where I met a nobo named Epic, a hyperactive guy of 37 (although he looks 22) who runs some kind of tactical school in Seattle, I was never quite clear on the details.

I stayed up too late giving Epic the obligatory "White Mountains" talk, so now it's time to get some sleep.

SATURDAY, JULY 7, 2018

Seth Warner Shelter – 11.5 Miles

The post office doesn't open until 9:00 a.m., so I probably won't be able to get back to the trail until 11:00 a.m. or thereabouts, which means I probably won't make it to Massachusetts today.

As it turns out, I didn't get back to the trail until noon. I met some nudists along the way who were doing a section hike, he superbly bronzed while she had shaved especially close this morning. Apparently it is completely legal to go around naked in the state of Vermont. Good to know.

I reached Seth Warner shelter at 5:00 p.m., and set up for my last night in Vermont. Two good looking female Long Trail hikers were at first going to stay in the shelter, but changed their minds after five college boys showed up. Aw shucks! The women went off to pitch their tent, the college boys tented out as well, so I have the shelter to myself.

SUNDAY, JULY 8, 2018
North Adams, Massachusetts – 8.4 Miles

Sometime in the dark of last night, loons or some other water birds began calling near the shelter, first here then there, loud ululations that woke me up from a deep sleep. I shrugged it off and went back to sleep, and was awoken again when those two Long Trail hikers came into the shelter and huddled in the far corner.

"What are they?" one of them asked tremulously.

"I don't know," said the other. "Oh my God, I think they're right by the tent now. *Right by the tent!*"

"Wha?" I said groggily. The two turned their red headlight beams toward me.

"What are those?" they asked together. "Wolves? Bears?"

"Loons," I answered, barely awake.

"Oh my God! What are *loons*?"

"Water birds."

"*Birds?*"

With that, I turned onto the other shoulder and went back to sleep. Hilarious.

I was up before 5:00 a.m., and got coffee going against an unexpected morning chill. It was seriously cold this morning, my breath condensing into puffs that lingered in the still air of the shelter. Weird weather.

The two Long Trail hikers must have returned to their tent, because I was alone again, free to spread out and make all the noise I wanted as I loaded my backpack and made breakfast. I was on the trail by 6:00 a.m., all the others still in their tents snoozing away.

I hiked into North Adams, Massachusetts at 9:00 a.m., and decided to make this day a nero. I am even with my last hike again, having actually been a day ahead as I went through Vermont. I'll rest and resupply, and get a fresh start tomorrow.

MORE NOTES FROM THE FIELD

MONDAY, JULY 9, 2018

Dalton, Massachusetts – 23 Miles

The weather is nice today, clear and warm but not too hot. After a big breakfast, I got on the trail at 8:15 a.m. and went fast, fast, fast, up and over Mt. Greylock, and then into Cheshire, where I stopped for a break at the hot dog stand. God bless that hot dog stand!

Four big hot dogs dripping with chili, and two beers later, I got going again, feeling sated and invincible. Before I knew it, I was making the one-mile road walk into Dalton and had 23 miles under my feet for the day. I threw down at a cheap motel, and while I was out looking for food, I met up with Mr. Hiker, who probably got past me when I was in Bennington. So we'll probably be going past one another for the next little bit. It'll be nice to have a sobo to talk to every once in a while.

TUESDAY, JULY 10, 2018

U.S. Highway 20 – 19 Miles

This was an uninspiring day, mostly flat and fast, but the heat came up again, oppressive, and this sucked all of my energy. I'm a mile short of the Massachusetts Turnpike, and just a mile past that is Upper Goose Pond, where I'm supposed to meet up with Mr. Hiker. Too hot, too tired, I'm going to throw down here instead and catch up with Mr. Hiker tomorrow.

WEDNESDAY, JULY 11, 2018

East Mountain Retreat Center – 21.7 Miles

Much cooler today, so with an early start I made good miles.

Stopped at mile 649.7, a country road, where some kids have set up a surprisingly elaborate kiosk for hikers. The kiosk has cold drinks, snacks, water, and a charging port for phones, all self-serve and on the honor system. I bought a cold drink then sat at a picnic table in the shade, marveling at the ingenuity of those kids.

Soon I was joined by a nobo from Canada named Ararax, an interesting woman in her early twenties. We shared stories, and then Mr. Hiker showed up. I figured that he was out ahead of me, but he said he stayed late at Upper Goose Pond for the pancakes the caretaker makes for hikers. I had forgotten about those. Darn! I missed out. Mr. Hiker then reported—having been informed by a nobo—that Whip had somehow gotten out ahead of us by a few days. I couldn't imagine how I could have missed him going by, since he was a day behind the last time I saw him in Gorham, but I'm glad he's doing well.

I left Mr. Hiker and Ararax at the kiosk and pushed on, and then at mile 659.9 I encountered a troop of boy scouts who were hopelessly lost. The adults looked beat to heck, limping from what were undoubtedly blisters, and praying that they were close to a shelter. I informed them that there was a shelter two miles ahead and another two miles behind, pointed the way, and wished them the best.

On Massachusetts Route 23, I caught a lucky hitch up to the East Mountain Retreat Center, where I stayed with Dude, Crispy, Kyle and the others in 2001. Lois is still here, albeit much, much older. She found the trail register from 2001, and we leafed through it together until we came to my entry from seventeen years ago. That was a special moment.

There is no one else here. Time for bed.

THURSDAY, JULY 12, 2018

Glen Brook Shelter – 17.8 Miles

I'm adding in the 1.5-mile hike from the East Mountain Retreat Center back to the trailhead, so here I am at Glen Brook shelter again, and on the same day, and I don't remember the place at all.

This was an interesting day. I was hiking by 6:00 a.m., the morning was cool, and I made good time. I reached the road to Great Barrington at 10:00 a.m., where a trail angel named Flash Gordon pulled up in a pickup truck as if from nowhere and asked if I wanted a ride into town. Sure, I said. I needed resupply, and I needed a new pair of shoes, since the pair I bought in Maine have finally come apart.

Flash Gordon drove me into town, waiting patiently at each store while I went in to buy the things I needed. I bought the same model of shoe, having hiked 555 miles on the previous pair while never getting blisters or having any foot problems. After a stop at the post office to mail the old shoes home—along with some other odds and ends—Flash Gordon drove me back to the trailhead. Even though he was a 2009 thru-hiker, and therefore knows the rigors of the trail, this was an incredible gesture, another bit of serendipity, and I was as grateful as I could express, which never seems enough.

A few miles on I met another trail angel, Vagrant Bear, a 1985 thru-hiker. He was serving cold drinks and hot dogs out of the bed of his pickup. I ate until I was sated, sharing stories with Vagrant Bear. I'm envious. I really wish I had done a thru-hike back in that era.

Went past the Shay's Rebellion monument, then climbed up Jug End, where I rested for a while and took in the view. I arrived here at 4:15 p.m. Mr. Hiker came in right behind me. There's another shelter full of nobos just across the way, but Mr. Hiker and I are alone here.

FRIDAY, JULY 13, 2018

Salishury, Connecticut – 12.7 Miles

It got cold last night. What the—it's July, man!

Out first and hiking by 6:00 a.m. Mr. Hiker soon caught up, and then we hiked together to the Connecticut state line, where he got out ahead during some climbs and I never saw him again.

I reached Salisbury at 1:15 p.m. and with plenty of time to reach Falls Village, but there's a woman in Salisbury I'd heard about who lets hikers stay in her home. Her name is Maria McCabe. From the interesting things I'd heard, I wanted to meet her.

Maria is 89 years old, with a slender form and a petite face. Looking at her you can tell that she would have been an extraordinarily beautiful young woman. She speaks with an accent, and I soon learned that she was born and raised in the Italian Dolomites when the area was still controlled by Austria. She was a child of the war, forced along with the other girls in her school to engage in Nazi propaganda. When the Americans arrived, she met one, married him, and relocated to the United States.

That husband passed away, so she remarried, and then that husband passed away. Now she lives alone in an aging Victorian house and takes in hikers. Her children live elsewhere. With her supple wit and surprising clarity, I believe Maria may be the most interesting woman I have ever met.

Hikers room upstairs. Maria can't make that climb anymore, so she handed me a stack of sheets and towels, bid me make up my own bed &c., and be sure to bring down the dirty linens in the morning. I met a nobo upstairs named Loner Boner, 77 years old and making his fourth northbound thru-hike. I was amazed and in awe.

Sat up late talking with Maria. She tells her stories so well that I wanted only to listen. Finally time for bed, I haven't heard a peep from Loner Boner since before sunset.

SATURDAY, JULY 14, 2018

Silver Hill Campsite – 22.4 Miles

Got up early with Loner Boner, and was hiking through the morning chill at 5:45 a.m., I going one way and he the other.

Flat and fast so made good time. Caught up to Mr. Hiker in Falls Village, but he got ahead again once the climbs started.

It was a nice but uneventful day. I reached Silver Hill Campground (where I stayed in 2001) at 4:30 p.m. So here I am under the pavilion, the sky closing in, talking to a flip-flopper named Whistler and wishing I had a beer.

Later—

A group of nobos were in and out, and then it began to rain. I'm sacking out on a picnic table under the pavilion. The sound of the rain is actually soothing.

SUNDAY, JULY 15, 2018

Kent, Connecticut — 10.3 Miles

Woke up at the usual time, hiking by 6:00 a.m. It wasn't raining, but the woods were dripping and humid.

Kept up a fast pace on that flat trail, met a trail angel named Tinkerbell, who made me a cheeseburger. We talked until 10:00 a.m., and then I pushed on again, directly into the steep climbs toward St. John's Ledges. I slipped on those rocks and poked myself in the left eye with a trekking pole handle. I have a black eye now, look like an old Tareyton commercial. I'm going to nero into Kent to help stage my transit of New York.

MONDAY, JULY 16, 2018

Pawling, New York — 18.7 Miles

I zeroed on this day last time, so now I can get ahead again.

The morning was cool, and I made good time despite the various rocky climbs. I left off my ankle brace this morning, having had nary a mishap since Maine, so sure enough I turned my right ankle in the rocks and took a hard fall. No serious damage, just a few cuts. Needless to say, I put my ankle brace back on.

The rest of the hike went okay, the limp eventually went away. The heat and humidity are back, as are the bugs, especially horse flies and those damn little eye bombers.

Reached New York Route 22 at 3:30 p.m., and hitched into Pawling for the night.

TUESDAY, JULY 17, 2018

RPH Shelter — 19.7 Miles

Went over the Appalachian Trail Amtrak train stop first thing this morning. Someday I'm going to get here on a weekend and take that train into New York City.

The rest of the hike was mostly uneventful, although rich in trail landmarks: Pawling Marsh and its long boardwalk, the oldest tree on the trail (or perhaps the biggest, there's that one down in Virginia, too) and of course Nuclear Lake with its nuclear mosquitoes.

The rain came on hard at 2:00 p.m. Hiked through it to RPH shelter and there was Mr. Hiker, along with a lot of nobos and one local groupie, whose mouth ran faster than a 78 RPM record. Mr. Hiker and I both ordered pizzas, that novelty of RPH shelter, then turned in while the nobos played movies from some kind of device, using a ground cloth as a screen.

WEDNESDAY, JULY 18, 2018

U.S. Highway 9 – 19.7 Miles

Last night's nobos were obnoxious, so sleep was difficult. Up at 4:00 a.m. just to get it over with, on the trail by 5:15 a.m.

The weather's better, so I had a good hike, except that there has been a relo (trail relocation) around Fahnestock State Park that completely disoriented me. I am accustomed to hiking through the park, grabbing a hot dog along the way, but the trail now bypasses the park. The woods above the park were torn up, as if a tornado had come through, and I think that's what happened, either that or a devastating ice storm this past winter. Trail volunteers had already been in to clear the trail. I haven't seen such devastation since that awful section back in the Hundred-Mile Wilderness.

The blazing continues to be poor, so when I hiked into the grounds of the Graymoor Spiritual Life Center I got confused and was out the other side before I realized it. Damn, and I wanted to spread some of Freewind's ashes there.

There is now a deli called the Appalachian Deli on Highway 9 just outside Graymoor. I stopped in for hot dogs, fries and beer, and was carrying my order out to the picnic tables when Mr. Hiker showed up. We talked for a while and then he pushed on. I stayed back because I really want to leave some of Freewind's ashes at the Graymoor Monastery. I'll hitch into Peekskill and be back in the morning.

THURSDAY, JULY 19, 2018

Fort Montgomery, New York – 6.3 Miles

Had breakfast at the AT Deli, then hiked back to Graymoor to spread some of Freewind's ashes. There is a hill on the monastery grounds with an expansive view toward New York City. One of the friars took me up there in 2001. It's a serene site that simply exudes peace and contemplation, with shaded benches and a statue of Jesus and Mary, which is why I've had it in mind for Freewind.

I inquired at the security office about going up there, told Freewind's story to the officer, and was told in return that this would probably not be allowed, but—and with a wink—no one would stop me if I went up there, and perhaps I could be discreet…

So it all went as I had hoped, and now, on clear days, Freewind has a view of New York City.

Leaving Graymoor, I hiked the quick 6 miles to Bear Mountain, went across Bear Mountain Bridge and then through the zoo. I love that the trail goes through the zoo, blazes and all. What a thoughtful, unique experience. I stopped at the concession stand for pizza and beer, and met a nobo named Papa J. We talked for over an hour.

It was now getting later in the day, short miles but full of experiences. I had already planned to stay at Bear Mountain Bridge Motel, where I stayed on both my previous hikes. I knew that Doug, the owner, would remember me, and I looked forward to seeing him again. I called the motel, and was shocked to learn two things: that the motel had been sold three months ago, and that it was fully booked. This was really disappointing, and also meant that I had to get moving since I would now have to climb Bear Mountain and put on about 7 more miles to reach a shelter.

I said my goodbyes to Papa J, and was about to turn off my phone and put it away when it rang in my hand. It was Bear Mountain Bridge Motel calling. They'd had a cancellation, and could have a shuttle pick me up in fifteen minutes!

So my tradition of staying here remains unbroken. The new owners are hiker friendly, with a hiker box, shuttles for resupply, &c. All the rooms are taken by thru-hikers right now, all nobos except for me. We sat outside at a picnic table, talked and drank beers as the sun set. They were a good group.

FRIDAY, JULY 20, 2018

New York Route 17 – 18 Miles

Didn't get back to the trail until 8:30 a.m., but made great time in great weather. I went over Bear Mountain first thing, while it was still cool. There were thickets of ripe raspberries on both sides of the trail, a real treat.

Crossing Arden Valley Road 14 miles later, I learned that there was a hiker jamboree going on at Tiorati Circle, only ½ mile away, so I went on down to check it out. The jamboree was sponsored by some 1998 thru-hikers, one of whom, Night Eyes, met Earl Shaffer on that hike. What an honor it must have been to meet Earl Shaffer on his 50th anniversary hike, also his third and last thru-hike.

I hung around for an hour, had some food, and talked to some other thru-hikers. It would have been nice to stay through the weekend, when even more hikers would show up, nobos and sobos, but I felt that I needed to keep moving.

Soon I was at the Lemon Squeezer, where I met a young couple out for a day hike. We took each other's photos in the Lemon Squeezer, then hiked out together, where they offered me a ride into Harriman for the night.

SATURDAY, JULY 21, 2018

New York Route 17A – 11.8 Miles

Short miles today. I wanted more, but I feel drained. It's starting to rain, and I have poison ivy breaking out on my left shin. It must be from that section of overgrown trail a few days ago.

SUNDAY, JULY 22, 2018

New Jersey Route 94 – 15.1 Miles

Rain, rain, rain, and of course today I had to do Prospect Rock and the rest of that slippery ridge down to the New Jersey line. I took it slow and steady, and only went down once.

Afterward I picked up the pace. There was trail magic at Wawayanda shelter, which revived me. The sun came out briefly when I reached Route 94 and the hot dog stand. Four hot dogs later, I shuttled into Vernon for the night.

MONDAY, JULY 23, 2018

New Jersey Route 23 – 20.6 Miles

On the trail by 7:00 a.m., raining on and off. This is a fast section in dry weather, with long boardwalks and road walks, but the bog logs and rocks are terribly slippery in the rain. I skated over a few bog logs, barely keeping my balance.

I reached Pochuck Mountain shelter at 10:30 a.m., went in for water, and found a tribe of nobos yet to break camp and passing around a bottle of whiskey. It's not my place to pass judgment, but geez—

"No rules on the Appalachian Trail," one of them hollered at me.

"You're right," I hollered back, except—and this I kept to myself—the turning of the seasons, which might cause y'all to miss Mt. K if you don't get a move on.

I couldn't find High Point shelter, no idea where they put the thing, so I pushed on to High Point Park Headquarters, where I scored a free coke from the ladies inside and a shuttle to a nearby hostel called Mosey's Place.

Time to eat hearty, tomorrow will be a big day.

TUESDAY, JULY 24, 2018

Mohican Outdoor Center – 31.9 Miles

I'm writing all of this from the Mohican Outdoor Center. It's late. It's dark. My hands are still shaking.

Mosey made breakfast, then she shuttled me through the rain to the trail at 7:30 a.m. I made a quick 5 miles despite the rain, stopped at Mashipacong shelter for a break, where I met Tripad, a nobo who was slacking (or slack-packing—hiking with a lightened backpack) southbound. Somewhere in this section, Tripad would meet up with some nobo friends of his and pass them the keys to his van. His friends would then hike to the van and shuttle back to pick him up. This seems like a lot to coordinate, but Tripad wanted to have his biggest day ever at 28 miles or thereabouts. The rain didn't help, but with a vehicle and a tag team, he was certain he could do it.

Tripad was a young guy, bearded, and a lover of tequila. With a grin, he gave me one of those little single shot bottles of tequila, which I cached in my backpack to enjoy later. We set out together in the rain, hiking at a leisurely pace and making conversation. Soon he began to pull ahead, remembering the urgency of big miles, and I was unable to keep up with him.

After about an hour, though, I did catch up to him when he stopped for a break. He soon began to pull away again, and I marveled that he could move so fast over the wet, slippery rocks that made up that section of trail. I studied his feet, the way he moved, how he held his trekking poles up as if for balance. He seemed to see a line between and around the rocks, and seldom touched the ground with his trekking poles.

Behind him, I clicked away, my poles catching in cracks here and there, pulling me off balance or slowing me a half step. And then I had a revelation. I held up my poles, one in each hand and parallel to the ground, sighted well down the trail, to the rocks and obstacles ahead, then balancing with my poles held out, I picked up the pace.

I was soon on Tripad's heels, keeping pace with him, sidestepping slick rocks, dodging, anticipating the best footfalls, and using my poles for balance. We were almost jogging. It was amazing.

We stayed together into Culver Gap, went into Gyp's for burgers and beer, then got back on the trail with renewed energy. The day blew by, or I should say the woods blew by. We made Millbrook Road in the lowering light just before 8:00 p.m., and moments later the nobos pulled up in Tripad's van. In the waning minutes of daylight, Tripad had achieved his goal. He broke out more of those little tequila bottles, and we drank in celebration. Soon it was getting too dark to see. They all bundled into the van and took off, and I had 3 ½ miles yet to go in order to reach the Mohican Outdoor Center.

Headlight on, I took it slow. The rain had stopped, but the rocks were still slick, hard to gauge in the dark. I had gone maybe a mile when I heard a crash in the woods behind me. Whipping around, I saw the dark mass of a bear coming toward me on the trail.

He was close. I clacked my poles, shouted, "Hey bear! Hey bear!" but he kept coming, now only feet away and completely unperturbed by my poles and the sound of my voice. I threw a rock, which impacted at his paws, to which he didn't even pause. I continued to clack my poles, and when he finally came too close, the tips tagged his nose. He drew back from this, and then nonchalantly turned into the woods on the high side of the trail.

I was puzzled by the bear's behavior, having never seen one so bold on this side of the country. It was a young bear, maybe four years old, but at least a hundred and fifty pounds or more. If we'd made contact, he could have torn my head off with one swipe.

I turned and continued, keeping a constant watch on the woods up and to my right. I thought I was clear, and then I saw his eyes shining eerily in the beam of my headlight. He was paralleling me, waiting for the trail to turn, an opportunity for ambush. I shouted some more, threw rocks into the woods. I don't think I hit him, but his shining eyes disappeared and then all was black and quiet. I continued on cautiously, came out onto some exposed ledges cast gray in the moonlight, and picked my way along, careful where I placed my feet.

I heard nothing, only sensed it—the bear was coming out of the woods and onto the ledge.

This was bad. I had a rock wall on one side, on the other a precipitant fall. It was as if the bear knew exactly what it was doing. Not panicked but definitely frightened, I started throwing rocks, backing away as I did so. The bear shrugged this off and kept coming. Never turning my back to him, I was able to work my way around the ledge and into the woods where, as I had feared might happen, I slipped on a wet rock and went down.

I scrambled for my poles and to get myself upright, certain that I would feel the bear's hot breath on my neck at any moment. When I got to my feet, he was close. I threw a rock that careened off his nose, which seemed to startle him. He drew back, and then turned up into the woods, again taking the high ground. I could see his eyes shining in the dark, waiting. When I moved, he moved. He was not going to break off, I knew that now. I wondered if my poles could pierce his hide, or would they bend? Should I try for his eyes or go for his throat?

There was a rounded rock at my feet, about the size of a bowling ball. I hefted it, keeping my eyes on his, and with all my strength, like a Highlander Stone Throw, lobbed it up at him. It landed with a heavy thud that I could feel through my feet, and with that a crashing through the woods and the bear was gone.

I still had a mile or more to go. I proceeded warily, turning around every few steps to make sure the bear wasn't coming up behind me. When I reached the gravel road to the Mohican Outdoor Center, I went right but kept my eyes on the woods, still turning around every few steps just to be sure. And then I got to the center, sat on the steps out front. It was after 10:00 p.m. My hands were shaking. I drank in one gulp the tequila that Tripad had given me, and then I went inside, locking the door behind me.

WEDNESDAY, JULY 25, 2018

Delaware Water Gap – 10.8 Miles

Everything looks better in the light of morning, even if it's raining like crazy. I had a good breakfast, then got on the trail at 9:30 a.m.

I made a report about a habituated bear near the Mohican Outdoor Center. I can only guess that people have been feeding that bear, that he was trailing me hoping that I would toss him some food. This is how people and bears get killed.

I made Delaware Water Gap by 1:30 p.m., went to the hostel but it was full of nobos, so took a room down the road. Food, beer, called Mechanical Man down in Smith Gap to let him know I was coming, then I got in bed and slept the rest of the day away.

THURSDAY, JULY 26, 2018

Smith Gap, Pennsylvania – 25 Miles

Today's hike was fast and all in the sun. I stopped in at Kirkridge shelter, where Tollbooth Willy had his conjugal visit in 2001. The shelter was full of nobos. I counted thirty-five nobos today, and when I got to Mechanical Man's house in Smith Gap, there were three nobos in his garage. I have never seen this many nobos below New Jersey.

I have stayed with John Mechanical Man Stempa and his wife Linda, the Crayon Lady, on each of my hikes. In 2001, the Stempas took me to the circus. John Jr. was just a toddler then. In 2008, John Jr. was racing BMX bikes, so I went with the family to watch him race. Now I am told that John Jr. plays guitar in a band. He'll be playing at a club tomorrow night, so I've made arrangements for John to shuttle me back so I can see it.

John took us all into Kunkletown for food and free beers—yes, free beers. The restaurant doesn't have a liquor license, so hands out free beers to paying customers. I met a nobo from Switzerland who is not going to make it, but I didn't tell him that. The rest of these nobos are friendly and well meaning, but I don't think any of them will make it either. It's simply too late in the season.

In the meantime, John is getting old just like the rest of us. He's bald now, heavier and a little gruff, but I'm not put off. John and his family have been a big part of my Appalachian Trail experience. I consider him a friend.

John has really fixed up his garage, with a hiker box, some fans, and a dehumidifier. It's quite comfortable in here. Better yet, none of the nobos snore.

FRIDAY, JULY 27, 2018

Lehigh Gap, Pennsylvania – 12.7 Miles

Short miles today so that I don't get too far away for John to be able to bring me back. The trail has been reloed off of the Superfund ridge above Palmerton, which has added some climbs, making the section slower. And, I learned, the city of Palmerton no longer allows hikers to stay in the basement below city hall. Another trail tradition gone.

I met John just past the bridge over the Lehigh River, had lunch in Kunkletown then kicked around John's garage until it was time to go.

Well after dark, rain threatening, we drove to a bar in Allentown, where John Jr. was set up with a guy on electronic drums and a girl for vocals. The place was packed, lightening crackling beyond the windows, but the music was good. That trio has some skills. I hope they're successful.

We got back late, the garage empty, cool and comfortable. I'm glad I shuttled back. I'm glad I got to see John Jr. again. Time to get some sleep.

SATURDAY, JULY 28, 2018

Eckville Shelter – 24.7 Miles

Got a late start at 8:45 a.m., said goodbye to John, then climbed up out of Lehigh Gap, picking up speed once I was on top.

I stopped in at the pub on Highway 309 for food and beer, then pushed on without another break. I reached Eckville shelter at 8:00 p.m., getting lost along the way, but then I remembered... Eckville is the cabin with the solar shower, just down the road from the trailhead! I stayed here last time.

There was a young section hiker named Penguin already in the shelter, and later a Spanish lady named Tortuga came in. I used the solar shower, which felt wonderful, then turned in, fast asleep by 9:00 p.m.—

SUNDAY, JULY 29, 2018

Port Clinton, Pennsylvania – 14.8 Miles

—and woke up shortly thereafter because Penguin, bless his heart, snored loud enough to make the walls vibrate. I eventually drug my stuff outside and sacked out under the picnic table.

Underway by 6:45 a.m., sleep deprived, I just plodded along, arriving in Port Clinton at 1:00 p.m. I took a room at the Port Clinton Hotel (same as last time), had some food and beer, and now I need sleep. I think I'm going to zero tomorrow.

MONDAY, JULY 30, 2018

Port Clinton – Zero

Mr. Hiker is here! He arrived yesterday as well, but we somehow missed one another. I met him hanging out at the post office, waiting for it to open. I sat with him and we talked. He has really refined his gear, lightening up considerably. He has a new pair of shoes coming in a mail drop, and then he's going to pull out.

I am taking that zero. I'll use it to rest and resupply.

Later—

Caught the shuttle to Cabella's, where I was able to do my resupply. They've got a lot of great gear, but I don't really need anything else.

TUESDAY, JULY 31, 2018

501 Shelter – 24.1 Miles

That zero is just what I needed. Out the door at 5:00 a.m., I had a hard time finding the trailhead in the dark.

This was a fast 24 miles. Made it to the 501 shelter by 4:00 p.m., where I found Mr. Hiker. He seemed to be in a conundrum about his finances and whether or not he could finish the trail. We ordered pizzas—501 shelter is another cabin, like RPH, close to a road and with pizza delivery—then talked it out. I tried to convince him to stay the course, described the rewards of a complete thru-hike. He mulled that over, then pulled out just before sunset to camp and be alone with his thoughts. I hope he doesn't quit.

Some nobos and a flip-flopper came in late, but a good group. Nobody snored.

WEDNESDAY, AUGUST 1, 2018

Rausch Gap Shelter – 17.5 Miles

This was a mess of a day, heavy rain in the morning. I was up at 5:00 a.m., but waited until 7:00 a.m. before hiking out into it.

It was a slog through the rain, but I made good time until I came to a long section of trail that was completely overgrown with poison ivy. I'm sure I got it all over me, so at a spring running down into Swatara Gap I stripped naked, washed myself down, and rinsed out my clothes, including shoes and socks. This took an hour.

By now the sun was out. I came to a stream that was flashing across the trail, and had to climb across on a fallen tree. One slip and I would have been washed downstream in an instant. Once I cleared this, I came to a massive beaver pond that had completely engulfed the trail. I had no choice but to hike through it—nasty—stopping on the other side to rinse the funk out of my shoes and socks.

I reached Rausch Gap shelter at 4:00 p.m., raining again and soaking wet. There's a section hiker here named Plodder, and old guy, and a flip-flopper named Mon Damon, a young guy. This shelter has been rebuilt since last time. It's nice, and still has the spring running out front.

THURSDAY, AUGUST 2, 2018

Duncannon, Pennsylvania – 29 Miles

I wanted big miles today and I got them, despite the fact that there has been a big fat relo in this section, which added a few miles and a few climbs to what had been a mostly flat and fast trail.

I told poor Mon Damon wrong, told him that this section down to Duncannon was quick and easy. I didn't know about the relo. I knew something was wrong just past Peters Mountain shelter, when the trail suddenly veered off the top and skirted down the side of the ridge. Mon Damon and I stayed together through most of the day, but I could tell toward the end that he wished he hadn't listened to me and had thrown down at Peters Mountain shelter, which is a hiker Hilton, after all, a nice two-story shelter with stairs and a porch. The water source is way down the mountain, though. In 2001, I remember, I didn't have the energy to go down for water, had to yogi it off of other hikers. Humiliating.

I ran into a line of nobos today, all young women. I couldn't believe it. Nobos. In Pennsylvania. This late in the season. I asked if they were thru-hikers, and the lead girl answered, "Yep, still sending em."

Mon Damon caught a second wind and got out ahead of me. I made it to the Clarks Ferry Bridge by 5:00 p.m., and then another fifty minutes to hike to The Doyle in town. Mon Damon was already there and showered. He must have really put on the heat in those last few miles. The Doyle is another trail tradition, but time is catching up with it. Still, the food is good, the beer is cold, and I'm too tired to write more.

FRIDAY, AUGUST 3, 2018

U.S. Highway 11 – 17.8 Miles

Woke up near 6:00 a.m., feeling pretty beat up after yesterday's miles, but better after breakfast and coffee. Mon Damon pulled out early, while I stuck around to do laundry.

Got out at 9:00 a.m., and made quick time through a sultry, buggy morning. Light rain early, then just gray and humid. Nothing else remarkable. Reached Highway 11 at 3:30 p.m., then hiked into Carlisle for the night.

SATURDAY, AUGUST 4, 2018

Pine Grove Furnace State Park – 27.3 Miles

It rained overnight, which made the trail a muddy slog. On the way by 7:00 a.m., I made good time to Boiling Springs through mud and the worst bugs ever. A jogger came up behind me quietly and almost got herself jabbed with a trekking pole. She mouthed some unniceties at me as she went by. What a dick.

Boiling Springs is a nice town, but even though the trail goes right through it, and there's an ATC office here, the town offers just about zero to thru-hikers. The ATC office was closed. I blew through town without pause.

There's not much else to say about today. I had lunch at Hunter's Run Deli for the third time (I love this place), met an actual nobo, and a kind of sobo named Boy Scout. I say "kind of" because I think he's really just living on the trail and wandering south at the moment.

I reached the park at 5:45 p.m., went to Ironmaster's Mansion Hostel, where I met the caretaker, Holly. There's no one else here, so Holly and I had dinner and then talked well into the evening. I think she's a little lonely in this interregnum between northbounders and southbounders.

I'll reach the halfway point tomorrow!

SUNDAY, AUGUST 5, 2018

Caledonia State Park – 19.8 Miles

Out the door at 6:45 a.m., Holly still asleep. Reached the traditional halfway point early, took some photos, then pushed on to the actual 2018 halfway point at mile 1094.9. The halfway point changes often, of course, because of all the relos and such.

I left some of Freewind's ashes at the actual halfway point, even though it might be hard to find this site once the halfway point eventually changes. We're halfway on this hike, though, and that's what counts.

The rest of the day just blazed (intended) by. I saw in a register that Mr. Hiker is still on the trail and one day ahead. I'm glad he stuck with it.

MONDAY, AUGUST 6, 2018

Pen Mar County Park, Maryland – 18.2 Miles

Hiking by 7:15 a.m. It's hot, sticky, and buggy as hell. I didn't think I was hiking well today until I discovered that I had gone 10 miles thinking I had gone 7.

Nothing else much. The PA state line is just over there, so I haven't penetrated Maryland by more than a few tenths. When I got here, I met a man named Oggie who snuck me a cold beer. I say "snuck" because you're not supposed to drink beer in this park. We were discreet, though, and that beer sure was good.

TUESDAY, AUGUST 7, 2018

Rocky Run Shelter – 25.2 Miles

What a day! Clear and cool this morning. A little muggy later, but not too bad.

I made amazing miles, reaching South Mountain Inn on the road to Boonesboro at 4:00 p.m. I took a rest on their lawn, then pushed on. This is the section with the free shower house just off the trail. As I was passing the shower house, the sky turning gray, I had a sudden impulse. I went in and showered, then, feeling fresh and clean and smelling like whatever body wash it was that someone had left behind, I backtracked to South Mountain Inn for dinner.

Sitting at the bar, I ordered Salmon Wellington and a beer, and flirted with the bartender. The food was damn good, the beer even better. A few beers later, no success with the bartender but feeling sated just the same, I got back on the trail—now dark and starting to rain—and made the two quick and inebriated miles to Rocky Run shelter.

This is a new shelter, a double decker with a skylight, and there's no one else here! I'm up in the loft. What an awesome, awesome night it's going to be.

ATC Office
Harpers Ferry, West Virginia

WEDNESDAY, AUGUST 8, 2018

Harpers Ferry, West Virginia – 16 Miles

And what an awesome night it was, lulled to sleep by the soft patter of rain and the croaks of frogs. I slept so freakin' well that I didn't get out of the bag until 6:00 a.m.!

I hiked a fast 16 into Harpers Ferry, stopped in at the ATC office to have my photo made and to sign the register. I looked up my old photos. Hmm...I actually think I look better now.

Threw down at Teahorse Hostel. Met Laurel, the owner, and her son Benjamin. Laurel drove me up the road for resupply, and then I spent the rest of the day washing out my backpack (it needed it) and sewing up some rips and tears. This pack is my Alaska Kelty. It's twenty-four years old, been on the AT once before as well as the PCT, Scotland and elsewhere in the world, and once this hike is over it will have earned its retirement.

THURSDAY, AUGUST 9, 2018

Bears Den Trail Center, Virginia – 19.9 Miles

Got up too early, and then got turned around in the dark. Waited at the ATC office for the light to come up, then found the trail and got going.

Moved out fast over a trail that was rockier than I remembered. The trail was mostly dry, though. The humidity went down, and there were few bugs. I didn't see many people until I got near Bears Den, arriving at 2:30 p.m. I could have made more miles, but why? Besides, I've stayed here twice before. I like the place.

FRIDAY, AUGUST 10, 2018

Manassas Gap Shelter – 22.8 Miles

Woke up at 4:30 a.m., upstairs for coffee and pancakes, then on the trail by 6:00 a.m.

Met a girl, Katrina, a day hiker. We finished the Roller Coaster together, sharing conversation about healthy eating and living, and then she had to turn back. I liked her, and though I barely knew her, I missed her company.

Met some nobos, Mr. Fill from Köln, Germany, and Crazy Carb. Nice guys, but they're running a little late, don't you think?

Pushed on through the green tunnel, hours passing unnoticed. Arrived at Manassas Gap shelter at 4:30 p.m., all alone, threw my stuff in, started unloading my pack, then looked up to see a copperhead in the rafters.

"Holy sh—!"

I got out of there in one fast, fluid movement that is going to leave me with some aching muscles tomorrow. I took a stick to prod the snake with, but the snake just slithered into a crack where I couldn't see it. I rolled a cigarette and blew smoke into the crack, but the snake remained unmoved. And then I noticed something serendipitous if not also incongruous: someone had left a brand new Coleman tent rolled up inside the shelter!

Seriously? I mean seriously?

So I set up the tent, moved in, and had a great, snake-free night.

SATURDAY, AUGUST 11, 2018

Front Royal, Virginia — 10.5 Miles

One of the principle lessons I have learned on the Appalachian Trail is never hike into Shenandoah National Park on a weekend, so I threw down early here in Front Royal, resupplied, ate Mexican food, then went out later for a big Chinese buffet. Maybe that'll be enough calories to get me to Waynesboro.

There's a new outfitter in town called River and Peak Outfitters. I bought some sock liners and some gaiters to replace my tattered ones. Nice shop, nice people.

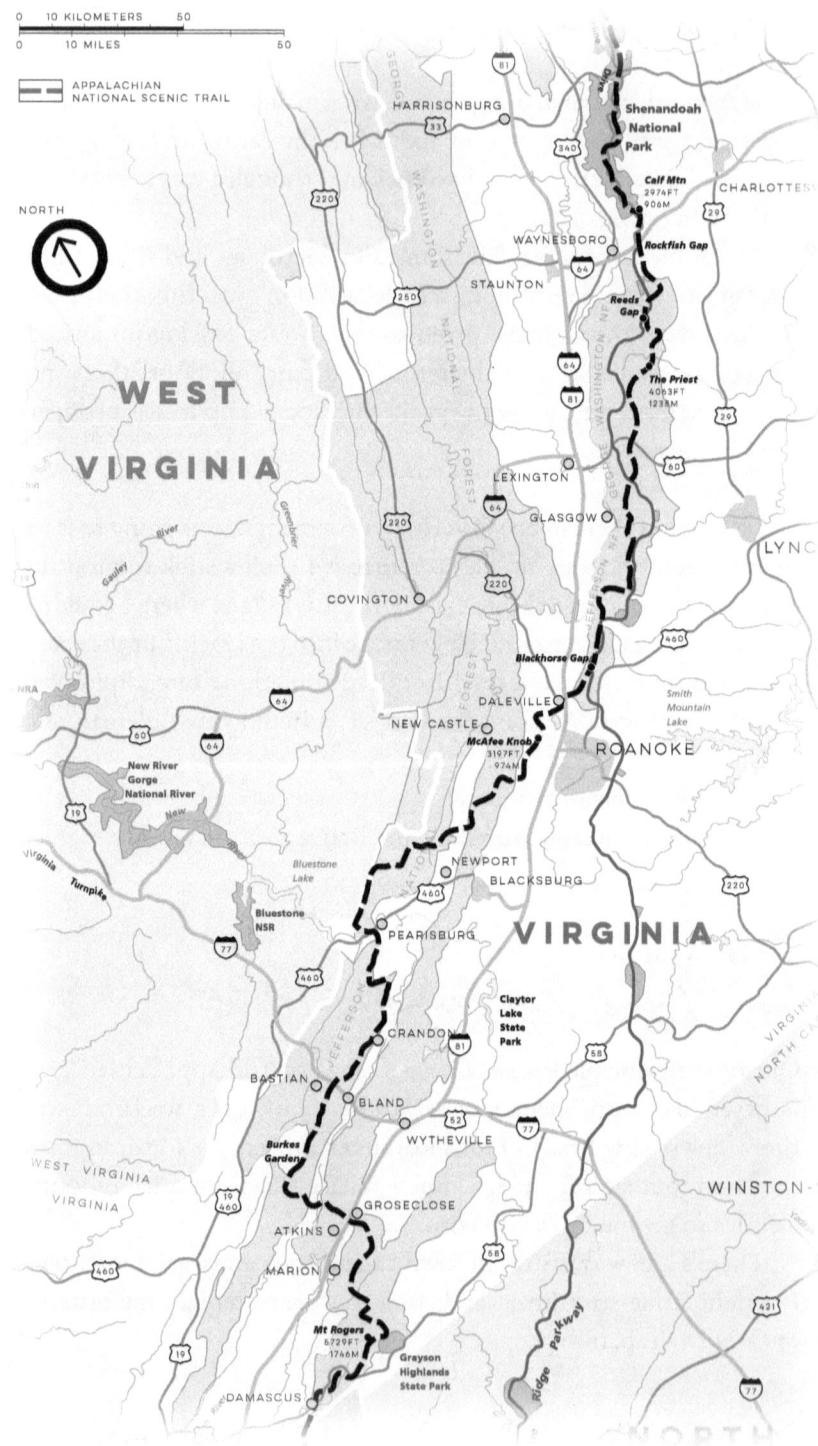

SUNDAY, AUGUST 12, 2018

Pass Mountain Hut, Shenandoah N.P. – 26.5 Miles

Didn't reach the trailhead until 7:45 a.m., but felt well and moved fast.

Storms moved in, though, raining hard and cold. My fingers were pruned and numb, and I began to worry about hypothermia.

The rain stopped by the time I reached the Elkwallow Wayside, but I was still cold, shivering at that point. Two large cups of coffee and two hot dogs warmed me up, so I pushed on, arriving here at 7:30 p.m. There's a flip-flopper here named IDHATN (I Don't Have a Trail Name). I think I met him up north. Nice guy, but he snores.

MONDAY, AUGUST 13, 2018

Big Meadow, Shenandoah N.P. – 18.8 Miles

Up at 5:00 a.m., but the light isn't coming up until after 6:00 a.m. now.

There's something different about the trail through here. All I remember from my previous hikes is a smooth, rolling experience throughout Shenandoah National Park. But this trail is rocky, the footing often poor. I couldn't understand how my memory could be so far off, and then it occurred to me that what I was experiencing was the effects of erosion. Perhaps some combination of rain and the increase in hikers has worn the trail down to loose rock. At any rate, these rocks are almost as tedious as Pennsylvania's rocks.

Stopped for lunch at Skyland Restaurant. IDHATN came in, so we talked and ate lunch together. I threw down at Big Meadow at 4:30 p.m., feeling weary and weak.

TUESDAY, AUGUST 14, 2018

Pinefield Hut, Shenandoah N.P. – 28.6 Miles

I soaked my sleeping bag with sweat last night. Have I been sick and didn't realize it? I felt strong this morning, though, and in great weather made big miles.

I met a nobo named Fire Goat while I was taking a break on Baldface Mountain. Great view, by the way. Fire Goat said she was committed to reaching Mt. K before October 15, which she looked completely capable of doing. She also knew Chipmunk. Remember him? I figured he had long since finished the trail, but she told me he had contracted Lyme Disease and had been off the trail for a while (this is one of the reasons I won't get into my bag until I have washed down). She then said he had recovered sufficiently to resume his hike, and was now two weeks ahead.

Onward, I met a PATC (Potomac Appalachian Trail Club) volunteer named Odd Bear, who was clearing a densely overgrown section. Odd Bear is 84 years old, has done three thru-hikes, and is planning at least one more. What an inspiration.

I made Hightop Hut by 3:30 p.m., debated with myself, then pushed on the 8.2 additional miles to get here, where I arrived at 7:30 p.m. In shelter with Jim, a 70 year old nobo section hiker, and Buddy, a 67 year old flip-flopper. Buddy is heading south and says he is also an early riser, so we'll hike out together in the morning.

WEDNESDAY, AUGUST 15, 2018

Waynesboro, Virginia – 33.9 Miles

A surly section hiker named Turtle or some such came in after dark, rattling around and flashing his headlight in our faces. What a dick.

Buddy and I were up early, but I got on the trail first and didn't see him again. Feeling pretty well, and in great weather, I set Waynesboro as my goal for the day.

Man, I flew. I reached the Loft Mountain Wayside by 8:00 a.m., stopped in to eat a lot of food, then pushed on. The day went fast. I laughed as I passed Blackrock Hut, where I was run out by the Boy Scouts last time. I was so disgusted with those scouts that I night-hiked out to escape them.

Curiously, I haven't seen a bear yet—but then maybe I've seen enough of bears on this hike.

Long in the day, I reached the side trail to Calf Mountain shelter. I threw down at this shelter near midnight last time, and found that I had caught up to Rocklayer, whom I hadn't seen since New York. I bypassed the shelter this time, though, determined to make Waynesboro. Soon thereafter, I hiked out of Shenandoah National Park. Someone had left trail magic by the tractor seats on top of Bears Den Mountain, which gave me the surge I needed to make the final 5.1 miles down to Waynesboro. I walked out of the woods at 8:00 p.m. Shortly thereafter, I caught a shuttle to Stanimal's Hostel, where I met up with Mr. Hiker once more, who, on the other hand, has seen quite a few bears, even startling a sow and cubs and living to tell the tale. He also reports that Mon Damon got off the trail in Harpers Ferry to take a break.

I'm tired from the big miles, but after food and a couple of beers, I feel as if I could take off again right now. Amazing.

THURSDAY, AUGUST 16, 2018

Waynesboro, Virginia - Zero

This is what I call a guilt-free zero, because on any other hiking day (including my previous hikes) I wouldn't have been here until later today. By making big miles, I get the "benefit" of being in town all day, which means I can resupply, do laundry and chores, and still have plenty of time to rest before I get on the trail again. Compare this to coming in at, say, 3:00 p.m. Now you have to hurry through everything in a compressed window. You don't get the "benefit" of being able to make your way leisurely through the day. That's my philosophy, anyway. Others may differ.

Mr. Hiker pulled out this morning. Soon thereafter, IDHATN came in. I'm calling him Idaho now, because IDHATN is just weird.

I wanted to go into the Bank of America branch here. In 2008, in Harpers Ferry, an ATM ate my debit card. I wound up hiking all the way here without any money. Janet at the Waynesboro BofA was a real trail angel. She loaned me enough money to open an account. I repaid her and sent my thanks after the trail, but I was looking forward to going back in after ten years, and if Janet was no longer there, to at least tell this story to the current staff. Sadly, the Waynesboro branch has been closed.

I have retired my third pair of shoes. The Great Barrington shoes got me here, 659 miles, but they have holes in them now, and have worn a water blister on my ankle. I now have my replacement shoes from Maine. Red and cushy. Let's see how they work out.

This is a great hostel, by the way. Stanimal is a thru-hiker himself, so he has the place set up perfectly. No sign of Buddy.

FRIDAY, AUGUST 17, 2018

Reeds Gap, Virginia – 19.1 Miles

Up early and hiking by 6:45 a.m. Met Idaho 7 ½ miles in, slack-packing northbound back to Stanimal's.

Not much else to say about today. I didn't meet any other hikers. There has been some rain, and these new shoes are hurting my feet.

SATURDAY, AUGUST 18, 2018

Virginia Route 56 – 10.7 Miles

I was dragging by the time I opened my eyes this morning, no energy at all. And it was raining.

I plodded over Three Ridges Mountain in the rain. No really, it kicked my butt. Slick and slippery on the rocky climbs and descents, depressed when I saw The Priest through a clearing and realized that I had to get over that today as well.

I hiked onto Route 56 at 2:30 p.m., the rain a constant, paused and wondered where I could draw the energy to make those thirty-seven or so switchbacks up The Priest to the next shelter. And then I saw Idaho lounging at the trailhead across the way, tented in his rain poncho.

"What's up?" I asked him.

It turns out he had just slack-packed The Priest from the south, and was waiting for a shuttle back to Stanimal's.

"No shit." I said.

And so in another bit of serendipity, I shared the shuttle with Idaho, and now I'm back in Waynesboro. Buddy is here now, along with another flip-flopper named Disco.

Now I'm ready to go to sleep and forget about this day.

SUNDAY, AUGUST 19, 2018

Cow Camp Shelter - 21.6 Miles

Shuttled back to the trailhead at 8:45 a.m., summited The Priest in two hours, light rain all the way.

I scattered some of Freewind's ashes on The Priest during a brief and sudden lull in the rain. The Priest is a major climb in Virginia, and is also visible from the Blue Ridge Parkway. Freewind belongs here. It felt right.

The rain started up again no sooner than I was done, but it didn't slow me. I hiked hard and fast. Idaho was slacking this section northbound, but I never saw him. Can't imagine how we missed one another.

Arrived at Cow Camp shelter at 6:05 p.m. The rain has let up. All alone, I bathed in the stream. Felt good.

As I recall, this shelter is full of mice.

MONDAY, AUGUST 20, 2018

Glasgow, Virginia - 25.6 Miles

I did have to fight off the mice, but still slept pretty well.

It was a long, wet day. Got going at 6:15 a.m., as soon as it was light enough to see. There were long easy sections today, but also some tough climbs made worse by the rain.

Reached U.S. Highway 501 at 5:20 p.m., then shuttled into Glasgow. It turns out that Stanimal has a hostel here as well. We used to stay in the old hotel, which looks now as if it has been turned into low-rent apartments. Somehow—and surprisingly—Idaho is here. His strategy to slack-pack in reverse seems to be working for him.

TUESDAY, AUGUST 21, 2018

Thunder Ridge Overlook, Virginia – 13 Miles

A lot of rain today. Miserable. Shuttled back to Glasgow with Idaho, and with Stanimal's caretaker, Texas Dreamer. She's a real character.

WEDNESDAY, AUGUST 22, 2018

Virginia Route 614 – 15.4 Miles

I started late and had a leisurely hike today. This was a sweet section, mostly smooth. I met some Natural Bridge ATC volunteers who were clearing blowdowns. Nice people, very dedicated. Later I met a section hiker named Business Casual, a super interesting guy who has moved in some pretty heavy political circles. Fascinated, I cut my hike short and went into Middle Creek Campground with him, where we had beers and talked until late in the evening.

THURSDAY, AUGUST 23, 2018

Daleville, Virginia – 28 Miles

Woke up at 5:00 a.m., and so did Business Casual. We had breakfast, talked some more, and were on the trail by 7:15 a.m. My pace was too quick for BC, so we soon parted with a handshake.

The weather was amazing, clear and cool. Something bit me on the back of my right leg, and it is still swollen. Painful, doesn't itch. A spider, maybe?

I reached Daleville at 6:30 p.m. and went straight to a Mexican restaurant, where I ate a lot. Got a room at the HoJo, which is recommended as a hiker friendly place, and it is, complete with hiker rates, hiker boxes, and great attitudes.

FRIDAY, AUGUST 24, 2018

4 Pines Hostel – 25.7 Miles

This is my fourth stay at 4 Pines Hostel, and Joe still doesn't remember me. Oh well, four stays over seventeen years, and with the thousands of hikers he meets...I'm not taking it personally. This is four stays, by the way, because I also stayed here during my bicycle Tour de Virginia in 2012.

Great weather, but a tough day with a lot of climbs. Had great views on McAfee Knob, and a lull in day hikers long enough to scatter some of Freewind's ashes. Of course he needs to be on McAfee Knob. It's one of the more famous views on the Appalachian Trail.

Audie Murphy Monument

I got to Joe's place at 6:30 p.m., pretty worn out. He tossed me the keys to his van so that I could drive up the road for a pizza or several, and beers to go with.

Back at the hostel, there are a lot of section hikers here, and a flip-flopper named Wind Rider, a guy my age or a few years older. Mr. Hiker was here yesterday.

SATURDAY, AUGUST 25, 2018

Virginia Route 621 – 15.4 Miles

Good weather again today, which was Dragons Tooth day. I hiked up with a Roanoke ATC volunteer named Bob Egbert, who was doing a visitation count for the club. He was an informative guy and good hiking partner. He kept up, and I learned a lot. There were a lot of day hikers on top, and what a great day to be out, perfect weather and Polaroid views.

The climb up Brush Mountain took it out of me, though. I got one bar at the Audie Murphy Monument, so called Joe and asked for a shuttle back to the hostel. My plan had been to go on to Niday shelter, but man, I'm kind of beat.

Wind Rider is here. He shuttled back as well. Interesting guy, a retired Navy engineer—a *nuclear submarine* engineer, the kind of guy I've read about in books.

SUNDAY, AUGUST 26, 2018

War Spur Shelter – 19.6 Miles

I hiked with Wind Rider today. He was dubious about making 19 miles, but I talked him into it, stayed with him all the way, and we did it. This might have been one of his biggest mileage days.

At shelter, we met Milo, a flip-flopper, along with Webster, a young guy, and Webster's dad. Webster is about to finish his flip-flop hike at Pearisburg, so his big day is coming up pretty soon. His dad is along to accompany him on these final days. What a great gesture. I'm envious.

MONDAY, AUGUST 27, 2018

Pearisburg, Virginia – 32 Miles

Milo got out before sunrise, and I didn't see him again until way ass later. I said my goodbyes to Wind Rider and the others because I was going for big miles today and I knew they wouldn't want to do it.

This section of trail was in bad shape, overgrown and with a lot of rocks—not the best trail to make big miles on. There was also another big fat relo in here, which added to the punishment.

This trail was a trial, the weather warm, humid, and mostly clear. I caught Milo at Rice Field shelter at 5:00 p.m., where he was throwing down, but with only 7 miles or thereabouts to reach Pearisburg, I pushed on hard and fast, only hollering at him as I went by, not even stopping for water, which was a mistake because I ran out.

Going down the ridge, actually sprinting as it was getting late, I came across a slow spring and grudgingly stopped to fill my bottles, which took a while but I was by then desperate. Then I got moving again, drug myself over an inevitable final PUD, and got down into the Narrows parking area, where I called Doc at Angels Rest Hostel.

Man it was late, night coming down, but Doc said that anyone who would hike 32 miles to reach her hostel deserved a ride into town. She dropped me at a Mexican restaurant near her hostel, where I consumed muchos frijoles y muchas cervezas, then I hoofed it to the hostel and went straight to sleep.

TUESDAY, AUGUST 28, 2018

Pearisburg, Virginia – Zero

This is another guilt free zero. Let me explain: I slept in, had a big breakfast, went for resupply, and was doing laundry by the time Milo drug in. That could as well have been me, but by pushing it yesterday I've had the entire day to relax.

Webster also came in, completing his thru-hike. He is now a proud young man, and we're all proud of him. Wind Rider also came in today.

I bought a bag liner because I expect it will start getting cold again soon. I also went to Doc's office. She's a chiropractor, has a very reasonable hiker rate, so I thought, why not? I feel very languid now. Good call.

There are some interesting people here, including a mother-son team who live in a blue school bus and have been wandering around the country taking photos. She's a photographer, Finny Hill Photography. Great stories. Reminds me of the sixties.

WEDNESDAY, AUGUST 29, 2018

Pearisburg, Virginia – Zero

Okay, another zero, but it's just too damn nice here and these people are really fascinating.

THURSDAY, AUGUST 30, 2018

Virginia Route 606 – 26.9 Miles

Hiking at 7:00 a.m., it took one and a half hours to make the climb out of Pearisburg. Afterward I made good time, passing only a few section hikers all day. I wanted to make Lickskillet Hostel, but a big storm blew up just 5 miles from there. Robbie, who runs the hostel, came to shuttle me in. I wound up driving with him through sheeting rain and lightning to Pearisburg to pick up another hiker named Valley Forge, and since we were in Pearisburg anyway, we all went to the Mexican restaurant to replenish.

On the way back, now late and dark, Robbie had a flat in the middle of nowhere. His spare was also flat, so I figured we'd be sleeping in the car. In what must have been good karma, Robbie flagged down a guy in a truck who took the spare into Pearisburg, filled it and returned. And so back on the road, we arrived at the hostel at midnight.

And now I really need to get to sleep.

FRIDAY, AUGUST 31, 2018

U.S. Highway 52 – 19 Miles

Foggy and damp outside, hiking by 8:00 a.m.

I passed Wind Rider slacking north at 12:30 p.m., reached U.S. 52 at 3:00 p.m., and had a burger from the store. The sky looked like more rain was on the way. Shuttled back to Lickskillet Hostel, just Wind Rider there.

Robbie has an interesting set-up. The hostel is an old clapboard church that he is restoring as funds allow. Despite its high ceiling, the place is quite cozy. He's knocked together a shower house outside, which has hot water, and a porta-potty for the privy. Robbie sleeps in a motorhome parked alongside the church. He also has an interesting story to tell about his life, fighting back from addiction and other issues. This place is his surcease from those days.

SATURDAY, SEPTEMBER 1, 2018

Chestnut Knob Shelter – 21.4 Miles

This was a tough day. Two steep climbs, a lot of rock hopping, and I've done something to my left shin.

Started hiking at 8:00 a.m. after breakfast with Robbie and Wind Rider. The first six miles were fast, and then a long day along a long rocky ridge. Got here at 5:00 p.m. Wind Rider got in ahead of me, having started his hike from where he slacked yesterday. A section hiker named Pilot came it at 6:30 p.m.

I have only ever hiked past this shelter, probably catching it this time because of those earlier relos that have added miles. This shelter is a cabin in the middle of a bald, with incredible views down into a perfectly round valley that was probably gouged out by a meteorite in ages past.

We spent a great evening. Pilot brought wine, which he shared. My left shin is swelling, though. I think it's these new shoes, which are already coming apart. They snagged on a rock today and I went down, probably hyperextending something, Hopefully I can walk whatever it is off tomorrow.

SUNDAY, SEPTEMBER 2, 2018

Atkins, Virginia – 24.1 Miles

Got a good early start. Left Wind Rider and headed out at 6:30 a.m.

My shin is aching, but I still made good time. The trail was a lot of ups and downs and some hellishly overgrown farm fields. A storm blew in and I got soaked. Finally, after a day in which I saw no hikers, I reached Atkins at 4:15 p.m. I'm staying in the same motel I have stayed in twice before, new ownership, refurbished, and now called Relax Inn. This is where Kyle and I stayed in 2001, when the demons were circling and I got off the trail, so it has special meaning to me. I am here a day ahead of my 2008 hike, and in 2001 I wouldn't get here for twenty-five more days!

Milo is here with a flip-flopper named Furnace. They're shuttling and slack-packing all over the place. No telling where they'll be next.

MONDAY, SEPTEMBER 3, 2018

Dickey Gap, Virginia – 25.5 Miles

Up early but the fog was so thick I couldn't see to hike until 7:00 a.m.

The trail was overgrown for the first 12 miles, which meant wet feet, but the grade was good so I moved quickly. My shin is still swollen, although not painful. Weird. Met a section hiker named Revisit, originally from Houston, Texas. She attended my rival high school, so we had some stories to share. Otherwise I met no one.

The last climb was steep, but I made it into Dickey Gap by 5:30 p.m. A pair of trail angels, Canyonman (a 2014 thru-hiker) and his wife Alice stopped to give me a ride. They drove me way up the road to a restaurant, dropped me off, then came back and got me when I was finished. Then they drove me way off the other way to the church hostel in Troutdale, where they dropped me off for the night and gave me a bag of trail goodies, snacks and such. What generosity. Gosh I wish I lived closer to the trail so that I could help hikers, too.

I'm alone at the hostel. I've wrapped and elevated my leg, but the swelling isn't going down.

TUESDAY, SEPTEMBER 4, 2018

Massie Gap, Virginia – 17.7 Miles

My shin is sore this morning, and now down into my ankle. Everything is swollen below the knee. I can walk without a limp, though.

Canyonman and Alice picked me up early and shuttled me back to the trailhead. There's nothing I can do for them but offer my thanks, which just doesn't seem enough.

At the trailhead parking area at 8:00 a.m., I saw a guy on a touring bike messing with his rear derailleur and seeming perplexed. I approached him, told him I was a bike mechanic, and asked if he could use my help. He looked at me, his eyes went wide, and he exclaimed, "*Solo?*"

"Do I know you?" I asked, then I looked past his helmet and cycling apparel, and now my eyes went wide as well. "Holy crap! *Fresh Ground?*"

Yes, it was Fresh Ground, the trail angel I met in Vermont! Vermont feels like years ago in trail time. What are the freakin' odds?

Fresh Ground had finished doing trail magic for the season, and had come down south to do some biking on roads near the AT. His rear derailleur was out of adjustment, and so he couldn't shift into his lower gears, which he absolutely needed in this hilly terrain. It didn't take me long to adjust it for him, and then we reminisced and compared notes. Damn, what a coincidence! At last we parted, I on the trail and he on the road. As I entered the woods I could hear him shift into that lowest gear. I hope we meet again someday.

Our encounters have been both trail magic, and the magic of the trail.

Afterward, I set a goal of reaching Thomas Knob shelter, which would mean a 21-mile day. No problem with the miles, but Thomas Knob shelter is in an area that has been closed to overnight camping because of bear activity. I understand the need for caution around recalcitrant bears quite well, but I also know that Thomas Knob shelter is a sturdy double decker with a ladder through a small opening to the second floor. I weathered the outer fringes of Hurricane Hannah in that shelter in 2008. I would certainly have no fear of bears if I sacked out on that second floor, so I decided to hike in despite the closure and take my chances.

A few miles short of Thomas Knob shelter, though, the swelling in my lower left leg was so bad that I had difficulty getting my shoe back on. Afraid that this injury might cost me my hike if I pushed on any farther, I headed down to the parking area instead and caught a ride to Grayson Highlands Inn.

I've never been here before, but the place is nice. The owner, Dennis, has been very helpful and supportive. Now I'm in my room, my leg elevated and with a cold compress, and plenty of vitamin I in my system. I'm pretty sure I have injured my tibialis anterior. I've never had an injury in this area before—I never even got shin splints when I used to be a runner. I don't know what this means for my hike, but I'm worried.

WEDNESDAY, SEPTEMBER 5, 2018

Grayson Highlands Inn – Zero

There has been no reduction in the swelling, although I am not currently in pain. It goes without saying that I'm taking a zero today. Dennis is going to shuttle me into Damascus, where I'm going to buy a new pair of shoes and some lidocaine patches for my leg.

Later—

So I've got my new shoes. This time I went with the Salomon XA Pro 3D, kind of an upgrade from the Salomon Speed Cross 4 that I wore earlier. These shoes look a lot tougher. I think they'll get me to Springer. As for my last pair, I only got 361 miles out of them, so I'm done with that brand.

While in Damascus I saw Milo and Furnace, who are still shuttling around so much I can't tell exactly where they are in their hike. It was good to see them, though.

Back at the Inn, Wind Rider is here now. We're going to hike out together tomorrow if I can get this swelling down. In the meantime, the food here is incredible. I'm ready for another burger, maybe another beer, too.

Grayson Highlands

MORE NOTES FROM THE FIELD

THURSDAY, SEPTEMBER 6, 2018

Saunders Shelter – 23 Miles

My leg is still swollen, but not as bad, and with no pain whatsoever. I have wrapped it with a compression bandage over a lidocaine patch. Let's see what happens.

    Later—

    Set out early with Wind Rider, keeping a moderate pace to protect my leg. No outstanding views in this section, but we had nice weather. We did see the longhorn cattle that we'd heard about. I used to see them all the time in Texas, so took them for granted, but they are a novelty up here in the Highlands.

    We reached Saunders shelter at 6:00 p.m., having pushed a bit farther than Wind Rider would have liked, but he's tougher than he thinks he is. And we have the shelter to ourselves, which is nice.

    My leg is swollen, but no worse than it was. And it doesn't ache at all. These shoes are awesome! I wish I had discovered this model back in Maine.

FRIDAY, SEPTEMBER 7, 2018

Damascus, Virginia – 10.7 Miles

Wind Rider and I both woke up early. It was nice to break camp without having to worry about making noise. We could rattle pans and talk as loud as we wanted.

    Made a quick 10.7 into Damascus, arriving before 11:00 a.m. My leg is still swollen but feels fine otherwise. We are both staying at Woodchuck Hostel, out for food and resupply. Wind Rider is thinking about getting a pair of these Salomon Pro shoes as well.

    I am now even with my last hike again, so I'll be pulling out in the morning. Wind Rider is going to take a zero. We're in the endgame now, so this might be the last time I see him.

SATURDAY, SEPTEMBER 8, 2018

Tennessee Route 91 – 21.3 Miles

The swelling in my leg has gone down considerably, although it is still noticeably puffy.

 I got an early start at 7:00 a.m., had 15 miles in the can by noon, and arrived here at 3:00 p.m. For 1700 miles I fantasized that when I crossed into Tennessee, my Tennessee family and friends would be there waiting for me with trail magic, as I have seen with so many other hikers. Well, that didn't happen.

 I had been aiming for Iron Mountain shelter, where I stayed last time, but rain started up just as I reached Route 91 and I decided not to push my ankle any farther. So I'm in a campground sitting out the rain, no trail magic, but I'm glad to be in Tennessee anyway.

SUNDAY, SEPTEMBER 9, 2018

Shook Branch Road, Tennessee – 20.6 Miles

The trail was badly overgrown in this section, which slowed me and, of course, soaked my feet. I wasn't up for that climb over Pond Mountain today, so I threw down at this Boots Off Hostel, a new outfit since my last hike.

 I caught a shuttle into Hampton, Tennessee for food and resupply, and found that a hold had been put on my debit card because of unusual purchases. This made me furious because: one, I was starving and had no cash; two, I had given my itinerary to the bank; and three, the customer service dude was completely incompetent. So I had to shuttle back to the hostel to get my other card out of my backpack, then shuttle back to Hampton, and now it was late and my stomach was growling loud enough to startle the deer in the next county. All of this ate up a good hour and a half. I'm closing that account when I get home.

 Finally back to Boots Off Hostel, well after dark and carrying a bag with six Quarter Pounders in it, all with cheese and all for me. They have a unique set-up here. The bunkhouse has a central island for gear, and then curtained cubbies for the bunks, like a sleeper train. Then they have a bar with microwave &c., frozen pizzas, ice cream, and camp supplies. The shower house has galvanized tubs hanging from above. The tubs have holes in the bottom. When you turn on the water, the tub fills and water showers out through the holes. What a great idea. Very refreshing. The only downside to the place is that some of the croo are dicks.

MONDAY, SEPTEMBER 10, 2018

Mountaineer Shelter – 27.7 Miles

Got an early start, and climbed Pond Mountain in the dark. This is a tough climb, which I'm glad I did not attempt yesterday. I startled bears along the way, I could hear them huffing in the dark woods. None approached me, but I remained on edge until the sun came up.

This was a long day of ups and downs, rhododendron thickets and marshy hollows, with no road crossings or other landmarks. The weather was good, though, despite the poor forecast I saw back at the hostel. I met a married couple named Shannon and Julie from Bristol, Tennessee, who are doing the section down to U.S. Highway 19E. Nice people.

I reached Mountaineer shelter at 4:00 p.m., just before the sky unloaded with heavy rain. Shannon and Julie came in shortly thereafter, soaking wet but laughing it off. Pioneer shelter is a nice double decker with a porch. Just the three of us, I took the upper deck. We cooked dinner together, shared stories, then settled in for a nice night when in through the rain comes a section hiker named Scott who looks and talks like the actor Frank Langella. The guy turned out to be associated with the ATC in some way, but his dismissive disregard marked him as a real dick, so we avoided him.

We were all sound asleep to the drone of the rain when a man and woman came in. They made a mess and a lot of noise, waking us all up. Unapologetically slinging their wet gear all over me as they climbed to the upper deck, I couldn't even get them to acknowledge that other people were in the shelter. They set up their Big Agnes mattresses next to me, which meant that I would not be getting any more sleep tonight. These air mattresses have become all the rage on the trail, but they scrunch and crunch every time someone moves, a sound worse than snoring. People who use them in shelters are dicks.

TUESDAY, SEPTEMBER 11, 2018

U.S. Highway 19E – 8.8 Miles

Nope, I got no more sleep last night, so I got up at 4:00 a.m.—making as much noise as possible—and hiked out of there. I think the only people who slept last night were the two dicks on their Big Agnes mattresses. I said goodbye to Shannon and Julie, who were also well awake, and ignored Scott.

The morning went quick. I arrived at Highway 19E at 10:00 a.m., the sky threatening, then turned right for the short walk to Mountain Harbour Hostel, where I spent a splendid evening in 2008. The rain started up as soon as I was inside, so my timing was perfect.

They have made a lot of upgrades to the old barn since 2008, putting in coffee and juice services and a full kitchen. I'm taking a nero here, so took a bunk in the loft. Shannon and Julie came in through the rain, not to stay but to wait out of the rain for their ride home. We laughed about the two dicks who came in last night, and then, at our most animated, the two dicks walked into the hostel, not even making eye contact. We laughed even harder.

The two dicks took showers, then retrieved their car and left without a word (thank God). Shannon, Julie and I talked until their ride arrived. We hope to see one another again, but Bristol, Tennessee is so far from Middle Tennessee that we might as well live in different states.

Later, a flip-flopper girl from Canada named Ridley came in to pick up a mail drop. I tried without success to make conversation with her. Strange. She hiked out, and then minutes later the sky unloaded once more.

Southern Bald

The rest of this day has been relaxing. I am now one full day behind my last hike, but my leg is much improved.

WEDNESDAY, SEPTEMBER 12, 2018

Greasy Creek Gap, North Carolina – 26.7 Miles

Hiked out at 5:45 a.m. and humped up Hump Mountain in good time, making the bald on top at sunrise. Magic.

This was a fast section despite the climbs over the balds. I paused at Yellow Mountain Gap to pay homage to the Overmountain Men, one of whom had been David Crockett's father, whom I wrote about in *Founding Courage*. I caught up to and passed that flip-flopper girl, who was no more talkative today than yesterday. I was alone for the rest of the hike, just enjoying the views and the solitude.

I called it a day at Greasy Creek Gap at 5:00 p.m., then took the side trail a mile or so to Greasy Creek Friendly Hostel, which is so far back in the woods that I don't think I could possibly find it by car.

It's run by Randy (Gadget) and Connie (CC). Gadget is a character, so many stories. And CC, too. There are no other hikers here, and there haven't been for a while. This is the lull between northbounders and southbounders, so I think Gadget and CC were glad I showed up.

This was a great day. I loved every mile of it.

THURSDAY, SEPTEMBER 13, 2018

Erwin, Tennessee – 24.3 Miles

This is the section that crosses back and forth between Tennessee and North Carolina.

Didn't get back to the trail until 8:35 a.m., but moved out well and caught up to the flip-flopper girl, Ridley, as she was picking apples from an old orchard gone wild. This time we did talk, even hiked together for a while. It turns out that she is an interesting, intrepid young woman, having done her hike alone and on a tight budget, and sensibly cautious around strangers. To save money, she mostly tents out, which is why I had never seen her in a hostel. My pace was a step quicker than hers, so I eventually got out ahead.

There were a lot of relos in this section, which added about 4 miles. As a result, I didn't get into Erwin until after 6:00 p.m. I threw down at Uncle Johnny's Hostel, where I met his widow Charlotte and gave her my condolences. I had learned way up the trail that Uncle Johnny had passed away. He had been a rascal, well known on the trail. I often think about the old-timers I have met during my thru-hikes, many gone now, new chapters.

Also at the hostel are Milo and Furnace. I guess they have become a team, and I still can't tell where they are in their hike. Ridley is here as well. She hitched in from a road crossing back a few miles.

Charlotte put me in Cabin F, a nice one with a cushy bed. I'm going to sleep well tonight.

FRIDAY, SEPTEMBER 14, 2018

Sams Gap, North Carolina – 24.5 Miles

Got an early start at 5:45 a.m. Climbed into the darkness with bears scattering and crashing through the woods. One did pause to growl at me, but after hollering and clacking my poles, he took off the way bears are supposed to.

It was a day full of climbs and great views, especially on Bald Mountain. I reached Sams Gap at 4:30 p.m. and then shuttled to Natures Inn Hostel, another new place since last time. The guy who runs it is named Taft. There's not much else to say. All these cute little cabins and I'm the only one here.

SATURDAY, SEPTEMBER 15, 2018

Little Laurel Shelter – 25.2 Miles

What a day of endurance! This was a tough section, and on top of that, Tropical Storm Florence is rolling in.

The rain did hold off until afternoon. By then, my feet were so wet from the grassy balds that getting rained on didn't matter anyway. Big Butt Mountain kicked my butt and I began to drag, reaching shelter at 6:30 p.m., and so weary I could barely walk straight. I'm alone here except for a radio-collared bear dog that is sleeping under the shelter. He looked hungry so I tossed him some food. At least if a bear comes in the night I'll have some warning.

SUNDAY, SEPTEMBER 16, 2018

Hot Springs, North Carolina – 19.6 Miles

I learned from trail registers that other hikers, including Milo and Furnace, are sitting out Tropical Storm Florence. Not me. I think it's exhilarating.

Up at 4:30 a.m., I had coffee and the last of my food. The bear dog was still under the shelter. I had a good, worry-free night with him down there.

Started out in the cool and damp of the morning, 6:30 a.m., and made quick time to Log Cabin Road. There's a hostel down this road where I stayed last time, and where I think Milo and Furnace are even now sitting out Florence. Up on Spring Mountain, it got cold, I mean really cold. The sky was layered in gray and black, the wind powerful enough to part the trees. No thunder or lightening though, so I pushed on with some confidence, keeping a sharp eye out for potential blowdowns that might fall my way.

Soaked from waves of spattering rain, and getting a bit too cold, I stopped in at Spring Mountain shelter to make coffee and warm up. With no food left, I had only coffee and sugar to get me to Hot Springs. I jumped in place and windmilled my arms, and when I felt warm enough I went out into it and hiked on.

Over Rich Mountain, I could feel the air warm as I descended. Although the sky was still heavy, the rain held off on this side of the range. Soon I was into that rocky, arid descent toward the French Broad River and then across the bridge to Hot Springs.

I hiked into town at 2:00 p.m.—man this was fast day, Tropical Storm Florence and all—stopped for food and beer along the way, then threw down at Elmer's Sunnybank Inn, a stately old house full of books and trail lore, and of course Elmer's stories. Elmer thru-hiked in 1976, and stayed here on his hike. He bought the place in the 80s, and it has been a trail tradition ever since.

I'm going to take it easy for the rest of the day, lounge around and read some books. I'm going to zero tomorrow to resupply and get ready for the Smoky Mountains.

MONDAY, SEPTEMBER 17, 2018

Hot Springs, North Carolina – Zero

Ran around this morning getting everything done, resupply, laundry, &c. Rain moved in this afternoon. I sat on the upstairs balcony and just watched it come down, kind of in a trance. Ridley showed up this afternoon and, uncharacteristically, is staying here.

TUESDAY, SEPTEMBER 18, 2018

Davenport Gap, Tennessee – 33.1 Miles

Started hiking at 5:45 a.m., two hours to get up Bluff Mountain. Geez, what a climb! The sky cleared and I caught Max Patch in the full sun. Views, views, views—if you haven't been there you just can't know. Snowbird Mountain kicked my butt, but more crucially, slowed me down and wiped me out so that I didn't drag into Davenport Gap—or more specifically, onto Green Corner Road—until 8:30 p.m.

I picked my way through the dark to Standing Bear Hostel, where I stayed all alone last time but this time not so much. Fiction is here, completing sections to finish his hike. I met him before at Boots Off Hostel. There's also Mowgli, cool guy but I'm not sure what he's about, and a scattering of others in the various cabins.

Now I'm tired. Gotta sleep. Nothing more.

WEDNESDAY, SEPTEMBER 19, 2018

Pecks Corner Shelter – Great Smoky Mountains N.P. – 23.6 Miles

Couldn't get myself moving until 8:30 a.m., so tired. On the way down to I-40 from the hostel, I ran into a swarm of hornets, had to drop pack and sprint to get away. I have more than twenty stings. Son of a b—it's because some day hikers let their dog run loose. The dog stirred up the hornets, then hikers and dog cleared out, leaving their mess for the next unfortunate hiker—me. This same thing happened to me in Massachusetts. Prior to this hike, I had never been stung by a hornet while hiking. Bring your dog on the Appalachian Trail, but geez, keep it under control, okay?

It took a while to retrieve my backpack and to leave warning notes on the trail, and then onward into Great Smoky Mountains National Park, trying not to scratch my welts as I went.

The climb up Mt. Cammerer really took it out of me, just putting one foot in front of the other as if I hadn't gotten my trail legs a thousand miles ago, or maybe it was only the histamines from all these stings. Fiction went by me, that's how I found out about the day hikers and their dog. He had talked to them when he stopped for a break at Cosby Knob shelter. If I hadn't been so tired and itchy I would have backtracked to tell them off.

So it's official: the old self-registration kiosk is gone. One is now supposed to get a permit online or else hike out to a ranger station. And on top of that, *pay a fee*. And on top of that, *make reservations to stay in the shelters*. Nope, not gonna do it. I'm a blur in the light, a wraith in the dark. I'm stealthing GSMNP. Y'all keep up if you can.

Reached Pecks Corner shelter at 7:00 p.m. as it was getting dark. There are three section hikers from New York in the shelter, already in their bags. I made apologies for getting in late, kept it as quiet as I could while I cleaned up and cooked my ramen, ran my backpack up the bear cables out back, crawled into my bag, and now I *must* sleep.

THURSDAY, SEPTEMBER 20, 2018

Double Springs Shelter – Great Smoky Mountains N.P. – 21 Miles

Damn if those New Yorkers weren't sacked out on Big Agnes mattresses.

Got going at 7:00 a.m. while the New Yorkers were still snoring and scrunching and dreaming whatever it is that New Yorkers dream about. This was a tough section, going past many familiar sites: Newfound Gap, Clingmans Dome, and Mt. Collins shelter, where my son Jarred and I stayed when we did our section hike in 2016. It's always disorienting for me when I walk out of the woods into Newfound Gap and over Clingmans Dome because I have been to both many times in my car. On foot, though, perspectives change, the world changes, becoming bigger, more mysterious.

The weather was incredible today, so clear, so blue, in sunshine that I absorbed with gratitude. The weather had been poor in the Smokies during my previous hikes, so I was really seeing all of this for the first time. Despite how tired I was when I started out, I felt enervated early on, especially after Charlies Bunion, which I reached after the first few miles out of Pecks Corner. Charlies Bunion was Freewind's favorite site in the Great Smoky Mountains. That bare knob of rock with its sweeping views is inspiring regardless, but Freewind had a particularly spiritual experience there on one of his hikes when, as he sat atop the knob, a hawk, wafting on the thermals, held position directly in front of him. His mother told me this story, so it goes without saying that I should leave some of his ashes there.

The side trail up to Charlies Bunion is often full of day hikers, but when I arrived in that beautiful golden sun only one man was there, a guy named Tom who, as it turns out, is friends with Shannon and Julie, whom I had met at Pioneer shelter! Tom recognized my trail name when we introduced ourselves because Shannon and Julie had told him about me. My word, seriously? What are the odds?

Tom was moved by Freewind's story, and as equally dumbstruck as I about our connection. He took photos and video as I offered Freewind's ashes to the sighing wind, dust against perfect blue. It was a moving moment. Day hikers soon arrived, though, so we shook hands and I moved on.

Now in shelter at 5:00 p.m., I am alone. My backpack is high up in the bear cables, I have my trekking poles at my side, and I expect to sleep very well tonight.

FRIDAY, SEPTEMBER 21, 2018

Fontana Dam, North Carolina – 30.9 Miles

There is an actual privy at Double Springs shelter, you just have to look for it. I found it this morning by accident while stumbling around in fog so thick that I had a hard time finding my way back to shelter. Would I had found it first, but that's the way it goes in the woods.

I slept very well last night, woke up feeling refreshed. Started hiking at 5:30 a.m., but I probably should have waited. I couldn't see a damn thing through the fog, while the blazing in that section isn't great. I kept my eyes just ahead of my feet, poking along the most obvious trace but still getting off on side trails from time to time. Once the sun came up I was able to pick up the pace, although the fog didn't burn off until late in the morning.

I pushed hard, ate the last of my food, and scared up bears throughout the day. A couple of curious cubs came too close, but scattered after I introduced them to some dense flying objects.

Push, push, push—I've made this hike before so I knew the miles, I knew the terrain, and I knew that I could make Fontana Dam if I stuck with it. This is the backside of Great Smoky Mountains National Park, crossing into the drier rain shadow, where the woods aren't as majestic as deeper in the park, and where day hikers seldom venture. I saw only two people all day, a couple of young women hiking up from Fontana Dam.

The day went long and I was tired to match, low on water because it really is dry on this side of the park, and then I came to the sign that marks the park boundary and I grinned. I did it! I successfully stealthed Great Smoky Mountains National Park!

I hiked across Fontana Dam at 6:00 p.m., hot and thirsty. The visitor center was closed, nobody around and no cell reception, but the water fountains were running and the restrooms were blessedly air-conditioned. I washed up in the restroom, feeling much better, and would have happily spent the night on the restroom floor in the comfort of air-conditioning and clean water if I'd just had a little food. I was so hungry I was swallowing chewing gum.

I heard the rumble of Harley Davidsons, went out and met two bikers who had stopped to take in the view in the amber glow of last light. These guys were cool. They rode to Fontana Village, let the people there know that I was at the visitor center, and as dark descended for good, a shuttle arrived to pick me up.

Now I'm at Fontana Village, showered, fed, feeling pretty well—the usual. I'm going to zero tomorrow, which should be my last. I need the rest, and I need to resupply for a week of big miles.

SATURDAY, SEPTEMBER 22, 2018

Fontana Village, North Carolina – Zero

This is a planned zero, but I feel so well that I've had to force myself not to hike out today. Just rest and eat, and get an early start in the morning. Say it once more, just rest and eat. Big miles tomorrow.

SUNDAY, SEPTEMBER 23, 2018

Nantahala Outdoor Center, North Carolina – 27.2 Miles

Hiking by 5:30 a.m., but got tied up in the dark trying to stay on the trail. The blazing is really poor around the dam. And what's the deal, by the way, with all of the bad blazing this time? It seems as if it has been off and on bad like this since New Hampshire.

Today went fast after the one and a half hours it took to climb up from Fontana Dam. Afterward I was on that jagged ridge, slowed only by the killer climb up Cheoah Bald, worth the view, but whew! And then down, down, down, down...more down, more down—8 miles of down and then at 6:00 p.m., just in time to get into the store before it closed, I reached the Nantahala Outdoor Center.

A lot of people here this time, not in the bunkhouse but at the restaurant and bar. Good company after a long day.

Got a text: Mr. Hiker finished today! Despite his doubts back in Pennsylvania, he did it! Congratulations Mr. Hiker from North Carolina, whose off-trail name is Burt.

MONDAY, SEPTEMBER 24, 2018

Winding Stair Gap, North Carolina – 27.5 Miles

Started at 5:30 a.m. with that tough climb up Wesser Bald. The sky closed in, though, so no views today.

The cloud layer remained low through a day of tough climbs. It was positively freezing on Wayah Bald, gusting wind and spattering rain. I took shelter in the stone monument until I felt warm enough to go on. From there it was a punctuated downgrade of 10 miles into Winding Stair Gap, where I caught a hitch at 6:00 p.m. into Franklin.

I'm staying at the Gooder Grove Hostel with Stickman and Zen. It's a peculiar place, but warm and comfortable, and with pizza delivery. Zen will shuttle me back to the trailhead in the morning.

TUESDAY, SEPTEMBER 25, 2018

Deep Gap, North Carolina – 24.7 Miles

This was a super fast section with easy climbs, but it was wet and cold all day. Georgia is just 6 miles away! I'm within days of finishing, but gosh it still feels so far away.

WEDNESDAY, SEPTEMBER 26, 2018

Dicks Creek Gap, Georgia – 15.8 Miles

I had planned 32 miles today through a section that's not too hard, but cold, sheeting rain drove me out early, plus I got into some poison ivy in Bull Gap. When I got to the road, I went right for a mile or less to Top of Georgia Hostel, where I met the caretaker, Vagabond. She is both caretaker and character. I like her.

The forecast predicts bad weather on Springer Mountain through Friday. I don't want to finish in the rain, so might do a short section tomorrow then shuttle back here.

THURSDAY, SEPTEMBER 27, 2018

Unicoi Gap, Georgia – 16.7 Miles

This is the day I finished my 2008 hike. I would like to have finished on the same day this time, but it's pouring rain on Springer

Mountain right now. I should finish on the 29th, which I will call close enough.

I slept great last night thanks to Vagabond. When a group of section hikers came in late, she moved me to a quiet room. Bless her for that.

Started hiking at 8:10 a.m., started raining at 8:15 a.m. and continued pretty much all day. I reached Unicoi Gap at 3:00 p.m., wet, cold, and shivering, then shuttled back to Top of Georgia Hostel.

FRIDAY, SEPTEMBER 28, 2018

Neel Gap, Georgia – 21.2 Miles

Didn't start hiking until 9:00 a.m., but blazed through 21 miles by 4:30 p.m. The sky cleared as the day wore on, cool and breezy.

I'm at Mountain Crossings now, the outfitter and hostel that is plunked right in the middle of the trail. The climb up Blood Mountain begins just across the road. I stayed here last time. Pirate really took care of me then, these guys not so much. I found my register entry from 2008, but could not find a register for 2018, so I wrote a note and put it in the 2008 register instead.

No one else here. I found out that Ridley is a couple of hours ahead, probably camping on the other side of Blood Mountain.

SATURDAY, SEPTEMBER 29, 2018

Springer Mountain, Georgia – 31.1 Miles

This is it, the big day. It's 3:45 a.m. Coffee, coffee, coffee, food, food, food—I want to be on my way within the next thirty minutes.

And I was. I climbed Blood Mountain in the absolute dark, so worried about the bear activity in the area that I did something I have never done before—I turned on my phone while hiking and played loud music all the way up. I didn't startle any bears, and none seemed attracted to my playlist.

It was still dark when I got on top, stars crowding a vast, vast sky. Wow. Sunrise was like a dream, gentle light diffusing through the woods. In Jarrard Gap, still plunged in gray dawn, I went past Ridley's tent and gave a laugh. I thought for a moment to announce myself but then changed my mind. Let her sleep and get ready for her own big day.

I made 16 miles by noon. The weather was clear and cool all day, so I didn't even sweat that much. Along the way, Woody Gap I think, I ran into a group of day hikers and one of them was Revisit, the woman from Texas whom I had met near Atkins in Virginia! We stopped to talk, marveling at the coincidence. Her hiking partners were speechless.

That roller coaster section between Gooch Gap and Springer threatened the last of my reserves, but I dug in with my poles and gutted it out, startling myself (and a few day hikers) with my speed.

Finally the forest service road, trailhead parking, then climb, climb, climb the final mile. This is not a steep climb unless you have hiked 30 miles before reaching it, and over 2000 miles before that. It was 4:45 p.m. I scanned the top as I blazed in. Alone, thank God. I dropped to my knees at the plaque, exhaled a breath I think I had been holding for a mile, then gazed out toward the view that never changes as the miles rolled one by one behind my eyes.

I scattered Freewind's ashes. Not all of them, some I will return to his mother. They have been from one end of the trail to the other, completing Freewind's hike.

I wrote in the trail register:

Solo, Headin' Home

Freewind is already there

What an adventure; what a journey! I'm grateful that I could make this journey once more and that Freewind was with me all the way.

Until next time, seksti ar er ingenting!

Ha det bra

ME→GA '01   ME→GA '08   ME→GA '18

SATURDAY, OCTOBER 27, 2018

Smith County, Tennessee

A month off the Appalachian Trail, these weeks have passed as nothing. It took as many weeks to hike from Pearisburg, VA to Springer Mountain, GA, but those 635 miles stretched perception into ages. I call it *trail time*, that peculiar dilation of days into weeks, weeks into months, and months into near eternity. In trail time you register every moment of living, practically every breath. I feel its loss as if it were the very life of me. I've almost gone back a few times, grabbed my pack and poles and headed for the door. I'm not sure I will be able to wait ten years until my next hike. It might come sooner or, outside of trail time, it might just seem that way.

Each of my hikes has been a different experience, but none as pronounced as this one, from the missing moose in Maine to the relentless rain. But the biggest difference was probably that this was my third hike. Knowing what to expect did not dilute the experience for me, but it did sow confusion in some of the others. Most hikers I met, northbound, southbound, flip-flop and section, were in awe that I was on a third hike. A few, though, demanded an explanation that I was never able to satisfactorily supply: that I loved the trail; that I wanted to hike every ten years as long as I was able; that this is where I got the ideas for some of my books—all true but ultimately unsatisfying for the incredulous. To them, the trail was too strenuous, too dirty, too full of bugs and bears and other things that bit. Once was more than enough, they said while shaking their heads. They couldn't understand me, nor I them.

Toward the end of my hike, though, I think I finally figured it out. Each of my hikes has been a journey. Taken as a whole toward the end of my days they might even represent one journey, but a journey nonetheless. For these dubious sorts (and they were of all ages and genders), I think the trail is not a journey but an *activity*, like a marathon or triathlon, something to check off a list. Perhaps toward the ends of their hikes they finally figured it out as well. I hope so. It's a lot to miss otherwise.

Physically, I have now documented the health benefits of a long hike, benefits that I have sensed and felt and struggled to describe to skeptics. I have tried to describe the whole-sense of well-being that seems to arrive on schedule when I finally get my trail legs. Trail legs, when your endurance suddenly leaps from one day to the next, and when you begin to, as I say, hike *light*, is probably a result of the whole, the first noticeable benefit. For me, this comes in New Jersey, or rather, after about eight hundred miles, when my weight bottoms out, I have very little body fat left, and I have almost certainly sweated out every toxin and free radical in my body. It is this whole-sense of well-being, I think, that leads to the depression many of us experience after the trail, as we feel our bodies changing back, as we lose our trail legs.

Before and after this hike, I had my doctor take my vitals and draw blood for a complete blood count. The results were startling although, at least for me, not unexpected. I lost thirty-one pounds. On previous hikes I have lost more than forty pounds, but this time I started at a lower weight. The more interesting statistic is that my weight bottomed out at 148 pounds, almost exactly the same as my two previous hikes, leaving me to believe that if I had hiked another thousand miles my weight would have fallen no farther.

The results of my blood work were equally startling: HDL (good) cholesterol way up, LDL (bad) cholesterol way down, triglycerides way down, PSA way down, testosterone way up, vitamin D way up. Other counts, bilirubin, glucose, WBC, RBC and platelets all remained in the normal range before and after. Combine these results with the mental peace and freedom many thru-hikers experience, and is it any wonder that many of us are drawn back to the trail again and again?

These are my final field notes for my 2018 Appalachian Trail experience. I have many people to thank, but that list would go on and on. Instead I will narrow it down to just this: a special thanks to Kim, who handled my mail drops, gave me a hiking partner, and drove me to the airport early, early one May morning.

EPILOGUE

Freewind

SUNDAY, JULY 30, 2016
El Paso, Texas

I'm still traveling, albeit in places I have lived before, places that have changed. I might have the right accent but I've lost the lay of the land. I need directions to get around. I get lost easily. This makes me a tourist, which is why I am still traveling rather than visiting.

Fresh from Europe and still in a travel mindset has given me the opportunity to compare here and there. Are we really different? If so, how? Transportation is the first obvious difference. There are no trains here, of course, no Metro, no ticket kiosks, no efficient intercity rail system. A disembarking European tourist had better be able to speak English and drive a car, or else have socked away a lot of money for taxis. While I used more taxis during this journey than ever before, this was due to communication issues, not a lack of options. Here there are no options.

On the other hand, here you can get just about anything you want at just about any time you want, especially food, so no going hungry in the wee hours, no subsisting only on sacks of croissant or brioche. And coffee…it's not controversial here. I had to laugh at a European couple I overheard at a hotel in San Antonio the other morning. I couldn't place where they were from. They spoke English passably although heavily. Perhaps they were German or Austrian, perhaps they were from a little farther east, nevertheless it was early and they wanted coffee. The coffee maker was percolating away right there in the lobby, but this concept was so lost on them that they had walked past it indifferently on their way to the front desk.

"*Kafe?*" the European woman asked timidly. The man seemed to have deferred these cultural inquiries to the woman. He looked as if he were about to bolt if the answer didn't suit. I knew that feeling. The desk clerk pointed toward the coffee maker steaming just a few feet away. Both Europeans looked over skeptically. Their eyebrows rose. "Just help yourself," the desk clerk said with a friendly smile.

The two looked lost, as if they had slipped beyond the bounds of the known world. It was all I could do not to snort, not to step in with some consoling advice. Instead I watched them peruse the setup, question it with their eyes, eventually take cups and nervously pour. They walked away then, sipping, still looking confounded. I contrasted this with my experiences in Europe, especially that first morning in Torino when I got snapped back by the guy in the cafe because I ordered a *cafe grande* rather than a *cafe americano*. So that's something better here than there, our ability and desire to look after ourselves. For all that Italian barista's smug attitude and self-importance, I could as easily have made my own coffee.

Other differences stand out. Their toilets are better than ours, although our showerheads are far superior. This list could go on and on, but the main difference between here and there is arguably the English language. My travels have reinforced my appreciation of my native tongue. I know of no other language capable of conveying such diversity and subtlety with mere words, no language with as extensive a vocabulary. Pronounce any word wrong in French, German, &c., and communication will cease. Brows will wrinkle, expressions will become perplexed. In many instances an obvious loathing will set in. Mangle English, though, and one can most often still be understood. Questioned in a foreign accent so heavy that English words sound like boiling oatmeal, a native-English speaker will lean in, articulate clearly, work hard to communicate, to be helpful. I have seen it; I have done it.

In the end, perhaps this is the greatest difference.

SUNDAY, MAY 19, 2019

Massie Gap, Virginia

Dennis, the owner of Grayson Highlands Inn, is so accommodating that I feel I owe him much more than his standard room rate and the cost of breakfast. I stayed here during my 2018 thru-hike, a lifetime ago although it is still as present in my mind as the day Dennis shuttled Wind Rider and me back to the trailhead last September. Dennis was up early then as today, getting the coffee ready, warming up the stove for breakfast. Give it an hour, and Rocky will be heading back to the trail and I will be heading back to the farm.

Rocky lingers, I know that feeling as well. Regardless the miles behind us, hiking again after a couple of zero days always begins with an inexplicable sense of trepidation. This evaporates within the first quarter mile, for me at least, but it is there at the onset. Rocky is absently perusing the aisles of the store while Dennis cooks breakfast and I drink coffee. She is looking for some crucial element, some bit of resupply that she knows she has not forgotten. Or maybe she's just ready to hike, ready to plunge into the living stimulus of nature and challenge, and needs to keep her mind busy in this quiet, predawn hour.

Dennis drives us in his truck. I ask to go along, to see Rocky off into the next chapter of her adventure. The sun has scattered the morning clouds, now achingly beautiful and bright, a cool morning breeze. We all get out at the trailhead. Rocky playfully colored her hair at Trail Days yesterday, and now the sun catches it like a rainbow. She shoulders her pack, takes up her poles. We say goodbye, happy trails and so on. She looks ahead, behind, smiles, and then her face draws up with focus, she nods, and returns to another world.

Dennis and I watch from the truck. It's not long before Rocky's head bobs out of view. Dennis sighs, starts the truck, and I have to fight against myself not to fling open the door and follow Rocky up the trail.

Of this I feel certain: I will not be waiting ten years to thru-hike the Appalachian Trail again.

ABOUT THE AUTHOR

Kirk Ward Robinson was born and raised in south Texas, and has since lived in every continental American time zone. He is an inveterate hiker and cyclist who prefers to travel and explore the world that way. His wide-ranging career has included roles as a chief operating officer, bookstore manager, stagehand, bicycle mechanic, and executive director of an educational non-profit organization in cooperation with the National Park Service. Robinson has been twice named to Kirkus Reviews' Best Books: in 2012 for *Life in Continuum*, and in 2015 for *The Appalachian*. He earned five stars from Clarion Reviews for his novel *The Latter Half of Inglorious Years*.

These days he maintains a small ancestral farm in the hills of Tennessee.

www.kirkwardrobinson.com

www.ingramcontent.com/pod-product-compliance
Lightning Source LLC
Chambersburg PA
CBHW030434010526
44118CB00011B/635